Pleasures of the Imagination
Samuel Johnson Illustrated
ISBN: 978-0-9933714-5-5

Pleasures of the Imagination
Samuel Johnson Illustrated
ISBN: 978-0-9933714-5-5

All Rights Reserved.
No reproduction, copy or transmission of the publication may be made without written permission. No paragraph or section of this publication may be reproduced copied or transmitted save with the written permission or in accordance with the provisions of the Copyright Act 1956 (as amended)
Copyright 2016: Stefka Ritchie, Barbara Fogarty, Ana Stefanova and Svetlan Stefanov.
The rights of Stefka Ritchie, Barbara Fogarty, Ana Stefanova and Svetlan Stefanov to be identified as the authors of this work have been asserted in accordance with the Copyright Designs and Patents Act 1988
A copy of this book is deposited with the British Library

Published by

i2i Publishing. Manchester.
www.i2ipublishing.co.uk

A Sketch of Samuel Johnson (after Joshua Reynolds, 1769) by Svetlan Stefanov

Contents

Statements of the Contributors	5
Foreword	8
Introduction	11
Peculiarities of mid-eighteenth-century Art. Seven Interpretive Tools	17

Seven Essays preceded by Explanatory Notes

Brief analytical notes to *Rambler* 3	26
Rambler 3. An Allegory on Criticism	33
Brief analytical notes to *Rambler* 22	46
Rambler 22. An Allegory on Wit and Learning	50
Brief analytical notes to *Rambler* 33	60
Rambler 33. An Allegory on Rest and Labour	64
Brief analytical notes to *Rambler* 65	73
Rambler 65. Obidah and the Hermit. An Eastern Story	77
Brief analytical notes to *Rambler* 67	88
Rambler 67. The Garden of Hope. A Dream	92
Brief analytical notes to *Rambler* 102	104
Rambler 102. The Meaning of Life. A Dream	107
Analytical notes to *The Vision of Theodore*	116
The Vision of Theodore, the Hermit of Tenerife, found in his cell	127
Epilogue	153
Bibliography	157
List of Illustrations	162

STATEMENT - Stefka Ritchie, PhD

My study of the life and works of Samuel Johnson (1709-1784) over the past twenty years has led me to the conclusion that there is an apparent lack of interest in the historical significance of science in the evaluation of eighteenth century literature and that of Johnson. I also became aware that the skilful way in which pertinent scientific notions at the time were woven into the texture of the literature of the period, revealing the vibrant temper of the Age of Johnson, had clearly been overlooked.

Adhering closely to the intellectual and cultural milieu of the times I found striking connection between post-Newtonian science and art particularly after Newton's death in 1727, although at the time of Johnson's death in 1784 the influence was already waning and Newtonian science was seen more as mechanistic rather than inspirational to art. However, it is evident that mid-eighteenth century art was searching its soul in the pragmatic teaching of Francis Bacon and the intuitive flights of imagination in the Newtonian approach to scientific discovery. This led to a distinctly more didactic than descriptive art style, more visual, bathing in colour and universal in its attraction to the senses. Moreover, the emphasis was on the affinity between various disciplines in pursuit of knowledge in a pleasurable way.

In view of these peculiarities of the period and in view of the fact that it was evident that Johnson shared the sensibilities of the times, I thought that some of his essays in the *Rambler* (1750-1752) lend themselves to visual interpretation. But such an approach favours inter-disciplinary collaboration and I am grateful to Barbara Fogarty, Ana and Svetlan Stefanovi who shared my interest and collaborated in this Project which is original in design and implementation.

STATEMENT - Barbara Fogarty, MPhil

I am interested in the visual arts and their historical context. My research has been in the area of the mechanical reproduction of oil paintings in the late eighteenth century, specifically the mechanical paintings of Matthew Boulton (1728-1809) and Francis Eginton (1737-1805). Boulton was an important industrialist and entrepreneur, and was typical of eighteenth-century leaders in his fascination with natural philosophy in all its branches, particularly in astronomy and geology. Eginton was his chief designer and innovator. Mechanical paintings were less mechanised and more hand-painted than the name suggests, but such was the attraction of industrialisation that they were marketed for the mystique of their reproductive process.

My interest in the interaction between art and science and the application of science to industry is shared with Stefka Ritchie in her study of Samuel Johnson. Stefka has introduced me to the multi-layered approach of Johnson's writing in using his encyclopaedic knowledge and interest in contemporary discoveries and inventions to enrich his descriptive vocabulary and the visual imagery in his periodical essays.

I find I share a pedagogical aspiration with Johnson. I enjoy guiding groups of people around an art gallery with which I am familiar. As in reading, there is pleasure in looking deeply at art from one's own perspective, but I think the experience is enhanced by knowledge of the historical context of the works and the artists to give a richer understanding of the original intention of the artist.

I would like to thank Stefka for inviting me to join the project and giving me the opportunity to become better acquainted with one of the finest literary minds of the age that is known as the Age of Johnson.

STATEMENT - Svetlan Stefanov, AFIAP

As a Bulgarian fine art photographer and visual artist for many years, I find that my sustained interest in the visual arts is connected with the way I look at the inner and outer world. Namely, I always try to catch that unique moment, no matter how simple or how sophisticated that could be. From this point of view, I may describe my work as impulsive. I let the vision be - rich of emotion classical composition, no matter whether in black and white, or in colour. Further, I value the digital art today as it offers an amalgam of challenging creative options. For this reason, I welcomed the opportunity to work on this inter-disciplinary project as it has allowed me to explore the visionary capacity of Samuel Johnson's allegorical pieces; and in the process I have been able to probe into new avenues of art. It has been a rewarding creative experience.

STATEMENT - Dr Ana Stefanova, PhD

For me, it has been a pleasure and a challenge to collaborate in this unique inter-disciplinary scheme on an international level as an amateur illustrator of the seven selected allegories written by Samuel Johnson. My special thanks go to Stefka Ritchie who initiated and inspired this Project, acquainting me with some aspects of Johnson's writings and the peculiarities of the eighteenth-century spirit.

When I first read Johnson's allegories from his *Rambler* essays, I was impressed by his broad-minded views. The more I read, the more I felt that no matter of time, age and belief, big-hearted and spiritually charged people round the world will always feel the pulse of life in these writings. With a strive for progress, Johnson remains always supportive of the human struggle for achievement in the act of creation that is deeply embedded in the human psyche, despite various obstacles latent within us or in the world that surrounds us.

For me, as an analytical psychologist, reading Johnson's allegories was also a fantastic voyage of self-discovery. I was astonished at his simple yet precise observations. His wisdom and exactness drew me invariably to the dynamics of Nature to search for balance within and in the laws in the world – be it natural or artificially imposed on society. Well conversant with the Light and Darkness in the human soul, Johnson, the humanist, reveals the crucial principles in Nature with so much love, understanding and respect. With the brush of an artist he imaginatively portrays the main archetypes: the loving Mother Hope; the firm and severe Father Labour who deeply concerned for our wellbeing and happiness, teaches us to work hard yet in a meaningful way. The vivid personification of Wit is that of the proverbial eighteenth-century jolly Trickster.

On the huge canvas are also various aspects of Anima – the archetype of Woman who leads us through the fields of never-ending Unconsciousness in the face of Criticism, Learning, Menace, Fortitude, and others. But the moral always stays the same – the beauty and meaning in life can never be found in the poles' extremities. Johnson tells us that as in the physical world and that of the soul - outside and within, one should strive for the 'golden mean' towards a balance which may escape us but can open up new horizons and help us build a brave new world. Multi-faceted problems cannot be based on one-sided principles and their solutions need to be sought in a diversity of aspects. Describing the Dance of the archetypes – the relationships among the characters and how the different principles evolve, Johnson takes us on a journey through his ideas in pursuit of his social credo – that Education is part of enlightened knowledge, and supported by Creativity and Wellbeing, can lead us to a Meaningful Existence for our own good and that of society. These, of course, are the goals of our present times too which makes me think how much really we need loving teachers of Johnson's type.

Creating and experiencing images is an interaction with symbols, a Mystery. According to C. G. Jung, the father of analytical psychology, to work with symbols is to work with the treasures of the soul, with the archetypes of the collective unconscious; it is a path for communication with The Self. It is my wish that by adding visual form to the stories, the integration of text and image can make the reader's experience of the selected seven allegories also more enjoyable, leading to a greater appreciation of the richness of the propounded ideas. As Johnson states that words stand for images of things, I shall be happy if my interpretation of his reflections brings closer to readers today his pursuit of everlasting Truth, or, in the teaching of analytical psychology – the universal quest of wholeness of the human psyche.

FOREWORD by Stefka Ritchie

Samuel Johnson was born in 1709 in Lichfield, died in 1784 in London and is buried in Westminster Abbey, next to his former pupil and good friend David Garrick. Thus, his life spanned the first three quarters of the eighteenth century. After his arrival in London in 1737 at the age of twenty eight, Johnson embarked on a writing career. Although his writings varied from poems to journalistic debates, biographical sketches and also a play (*Irene*), it can be said that the essay format was favoured by him. His *Rambler* essays (1750-1752) were followed by those in the *Adventurer* (1752-1754) and the *Idler* (1758-1760). The *Rambler* essays came out anonymously and were printed twice weekly on Tuesdays and Saturdays, starting on Tuesday March 20, 1750 and finishing on Saturday March 14, 1752. Only on two occasions did Johnson revise the essays, first, for the 1752 folio edition in six volumes printed by Edward Cave, the editor of the *Gentleman's Magazine* to whom Johnson had assigned the copyright and second, for the fourth edition of 1756 in four volumes. The latter is the accepted official copy-text today and the present compilation adheres to this too. Thanks to the Internet, all two hundred and eight *Rambler* essays can now be easily accessed on the net.

By the time Johnson came to write the *Rambler* he was in his early forties and was engaged in the writing of *The Dictionary* (1746-1755). All but four of the 208 essays were written by Johnson who was particularly influenced as an essay writer by Sir Francis Bacon (1561-1626) whom he admired for his breadth of knowledge. The word 'essay' is derived from French ['essayer'] and in *The Dictionary* Johnson denoted it as an attempt or endeavour that related more to 'a trial or a first experiment'. This suggested not an orderly, but an irregular composition, which he likened to 'a loose sally of the mind', and supported his definition with an illustrative quotation from Bacon that reads, 'My *essays*, of all my other works, have been most current', alluding to the 'raw' characteristic of the essay as a type of writing 'still in progress', not yet finalised. No doubt, the nature of immediacy in the essay allowed Johnson to engage with a variety of topics and express his opinion on different often thorny issues of contemporary mid-eighteenth-century life from the cruelty of parental control to the folly and misery of a spendthrift, and the dubious virtues of marriage. To his reflections on more mundane every-day issues he added those on art and literary criticism.

On the whole, The *Rambler* essays were morally fired as through them Johnson hoped to enlighten the reader in an accessible and pleasant way. To do so, he chose to vary the literary form and on occasions favoured the allegory. In *The Dictionary*, 'allegory' is defined as 'a figurative discourse, in which something other is intended than is contained in the words literally taken; as, *wealth is the daughter of diligence, and the parent of authority*'. This suggests a hidden meaning which needs to be interpreted. Three of the selected *Rambler* pieces in the illustrated compilation presented here are allegories, namely: No 3, 'An Allegory on Criticism'; No 22, 'An allegory on Wit and Learning' and No 33, 'An allegorical history of Rest and Labour'. Further than that, Johnson used at times the notion of dream/vision, which, as he explains in *The Dictionary*, is a derivative from Dutch (droom), and represents something which really does not happen; it is 'a phantasm of a sleeping man', and for this it is considered to have more ingenuity than truth. Thus, this literary mode of writing demanded from the writer artistic imagination which Johnson truly displays in the four compositions featured here, *Rambler* No 65, 'Obdibah and the Hermit, an Eastern story'; No 67, 'The Garden of Hope, a dream'; No 102, 'The Voyage of Life' as well as *The Vision of Theodore* (1748) which was included in *The Preceptor of* 1749 and which Johnson valued as the best he ever wrote.

The present *Project* is a result of the shared response of four people: Barbara Fogarty, Stefka Ritchie, Ana Stefanova and Svetlan Stefanov. The Project is a unique collaborative inter-disciplinary endeavour.

Barbara Fogarty is a researcher in eighteenth-century history of art. Her Master of Philosophy thesis was written on Matthew Boulton and Francis Eginton's mechanical paintings 1777-1781, which explored the eighteenth century's fascination with the industrial reproduction of art. Barbara responded to the allegory and visual imagery of Johnson's essays and was encouraged to make parallels with early eighteenth-century artistic thinking and practice.

Stefka Ritchie has spent many years researching Samuel Johnson and his writings. Her study of Johnson's interest in matters of science, with particular attention to the influence of Bacon and Newton, was followed by further research on Johnson as a promoter of social improvement. Stefka believes that the modern reader today needs to have preliminary awareness of the peculiarities of the times in which Johnson lived in order to appreciate the embedded artistic skill in his essays, and has outlined seven interpretive tools.

Dr Ana Stefanova, the main illustrator here, is a Bulgarian medical doctor, psychologist, a researcher in folk psychology and an amateur artist. As a psychologist, Dr Stefanova likens her reading of Johnson's allegories to a fantastic voyage of discovery. The simple, yet precise observations, despite the centuries-gap have a common thread in all stories with a contemporary slant; in that one should strive for the 'golden mean' towards a balance which often escapes us but at the same time it can open up new horizons in our strife towards a better world.

Svetlan Stefanov is a digital artist and photographer and a winner of a number of international photographic exhibitions. Svetlan's extensive portfolio confirms that he likes to combine computer art and painting technique in an attempt to increase the aesthetic power of photography. Thus, always searching for new provocative ways of using the visual arts, he agreed to be the artistic designer of the present Project, seeing it as a challenging opportunity of an inter-disciplinary collaboration.

Initially, seven interpretive tools are outlined to provide the readers with ancillary ammunition to facilitate their better understanding of Johnson's expressive style of writing. Each of the seven pieces is preceded by explanatory notes in which these tools have been applied.

Notably, it is in the March issue of the *Gentleman's Magazine* (Vol. XX, 1750, p. 127) where there appears an advertisement of The *Rambler* 'to be published on Tuesday and Saturdays' in the following way: 'The writer makes his first address, Tuesday March 20, by a series of observations on the difficulty of doing it with advantage on any new occasion; a difficulty which, he says, is felt by every man, in his first transaction with the world, and confessed by the settled and popular forms of salutation, which necessity has introduced into all languages'. The statement leaves no doubt that The *Rambler* essays were launched anonymously by Johnson in the *Gentleman's Magazine*. Further, in the same issue of the *Gentleman's Magazine*, namely Vol. XX, 1750, on the same page (p. 127) is mentioned The *Rambler* No 2, Sat. 24 which is followed by a brief summary of it. Then comes an announcement of The *Rambler* No 3, Tuesday 27, with a resume of the essay that reads: '[The essay] proceeds to consider which is the proper business of an author, the difficulties that necessity attend the execution of it with success, and the inexcusable malevolence of those who wantonly obstruct those advances to reputation which must be made "with such expense of time and thought, by such slow degrees, with so great hazard in the miscarriage and so little advantage in the success". Against these persons who assume the name of Criticks he objects, that they cannot act against him by lawful authority; that they have presumed upon a forged commission, stiling [sic] themselves the ministers of Criticism without being able to produce any authentic evidence of delegation. To support this objection, he produces the following allegory, which concludes the paper'. The *Rambler* No 3 appears anonymously in full immediately after that (pp.128-130).

Interestingly, in the same year of 1750, in the *Gentleman's Magazine*, *Rambler* No 22 is printed on pp. 261-63 (June)*; *Rambler* No 33, Labour and Rest on pp. 320-22 (July)*; *Rambler* No 44, Modish Female Education, on pp. 368-70 (Aug.); *Rambler* No 54, Medication on the Vanity of human Life, pp. 415-17 (Sept.); *Rambler* No 67, The garden of Hope, pp. 512-14*; *Rambler* No 79, Fraud and Suspicious Mind, pp. 560-62. All those marked with an asterisk here are featured in the present compilation. The inclusion of the selected periodical essays would have had an advertising purpose aiming to awaken and sustain the readers' interest in The *Rambler*. It is widely accepted that Johnson wrote extensively as a hack writer for the *Gentleman's Magazine* and although the entire number of his contributions could never be fully known, there is certainly more scope for scholarly research in this area, as Emily Lorraine de Montluzin argues in 'Attributions to Authorship in the Gentleman's Magazine 1738-1868: An Electronic Union List' [online], www.bsuva.org.

All frontispieces in the present publication preceding the explanatory notes to the essays (with the exception of The *Vision of Theodore*) are befittingly frontispieces from the *Gentleman's Magazine* mainly during the years of Johnson's involvement with the journal, whereas the second frontispiece immediately before the essay text is on a modern theme and is the art work of Svetlan Stefanov.

INTRODUCTION by Barbara Fogarty

> The poet who knows most, will have the power of diversifying his scenes,
> And of gratifying the reader with remote allusions
> And unexpected instructions in a most imaginative way
> That lends itself to visual representation.
> Samuel Johnson, *Rasselas* (1759)

Many of Samuel Johnson's writings are so full of imagery that they invite a comparison with visual art seeking to establish the common influences on both artistic forms. This Introduction looks at historical links between art and literature and Johnson's friends and contacts with the art world. It also considers Johnson's own thoughts on the differences between poetry and painting and his favoured rhetoric of allegory as a literary form in some of his essays. Finally the added value of the illustrations is studied in relation to visualisation, response and interpretation for the modern audience.

Historical Parallels between Literature and Art

Art and Literature have a complex relationship; at any one time they may be expressing the same *zeitgeist* or being inspired by each other in the latest genres and styles. The most highly regarded genre of Western art from the Renaissance to the nineteenth century is considered to be history painting, namely idealised compositions of religious, historical or allegorical figures. Early in the eighteenth century, the artist and author Jonathan Richardson, in his *Essay on the Theory of Painting* (1715), emphasised the parallel between history painting and epic poetry in saying that, 'to paint a History, a Man ought to have the main qualities of a good Historian ... and have the Talents requisite to be a good poet; the rules for the Conduct of a Picture being much the same with those to be observed in writing a poem'. Other genres in diminishing order of importance were portraits, low-life scenes, still life and landscapes. The prevailing European styles at the beginning of the eighteenth century were the heavy theatrical Baroque art, the lighter more playful Rococo design from the Versailles court and the classical style of the art academies. However, the Age of Enlightenment in the mid-eighteenth century challenged these traditions by bringing secularism to art while towards the latter part of the century the Romantic poets succeeded in evoking an expressive mood in landscape painting.

Britain, at the time of Samuel Johnson that is the first three-quarters of the eighteenth century, did not have a recognisable artistic style until after the Royal Academy was established in 1768. There was a market for domestically produced portraits and topographical landscapes to parade the status of the owner but for high value art the British aristocracy flocked to the continent on the Grand Tour, or attracted Italian artists such as Canaletto to come to Britain. There were notable exceptions; in the early half of the century. William Hogarth (1697-1764) was painting and making prints of moral tales of hypocrisy, exploitation and downfall such as *A Harlot's Progress* (1733) and *Marriage à-la-mode* (c.1743); they had their parallel in *Moll Flanders* (1722) by Daniel Defoe (1660-1731) and *Pamela: or, Virtue Rewarded* (1740) written by Johnson's friend Samuel Richardson (1689-1761). But, Hogarth's characters Moll Hackabout and the young Earl and Countess Squander do not have the happy endings of these literary heroines. This was what Hogarth described as his 'War with the Connoisseurs' who wanted art to remain elitist. The accessibility of prints, in terms of cost and visibility in shops and taverns, democratised art in the same way that Johnson's *Rambler* essays (1750-52) made his writings on broader topics available to a wider public. Both Hogarth and Johnson wanted to reach and educate a wider audience with contemporary issues and that begins to pervade various forms of art after the middle of the eighteenth century.

Samuel Johnson and Art

Johnson's interest in art has been often questioned and it could be that his appreciation was not fully awakened until his friendship with the artist Joshua Reynolds (1732-92) in about 1756 when they both became members of the Society for the Encouragement of Arts, Manufactures and Commerce, for short the Society of Arts. The Society's members included also Hogarth, the Scottish portrait painter Allan Ramsay, the equine artist George Stubbs and the sculptor Louis-François Roubiliac.

Johnson's attachment to Reynolds was very strong and Johnson declared him 'almost the only man whom I call a friend'. Reynolds had returned from Italy in 1753 and rapidly became the leading portrait painter in London. His poses, which referenced classical sculpture and Old Master paintings, aimed to elevate the sitter rather than portray a striking likeness. A good example is the portrait of *Sarah Siddons as the Tragic Muse* (1784). The renowned actress strikes a pose, half turning on her throne, while in the shadows behind her lurk the two allegories of Pity and Terror. William Vaughan, in his book *British Painting: The Golden Age from Hogarth to Turner* (1999), commented that Reynolds and Johnson share a common style, which 'while classically based, is also related to a tradition of empirical common sense'. More than that, Reynolds here is giving a commoner a prominent position, and is resorting to the use of the personified figures of Pity and Terror, an artistic device that would be favoured also by Johnson. In 1768 Reynolds was a founder member and the first president of the Royal Academy of Arts (RA), and the following year Johnson became an honorary professor in ancient literature at the RA. He attended Reynolds' presidential lectures and helped him when these were published as *Discourses*. Reynolds had decided views on the use of allegory in context, and praised Nicolas Poussin's allegorical figures of different characters stressing that 'nothing in the picture ought to remind us of modern times' which would take away from the universality of the meaning (*Discourses 1772*). He only allowed the Flemish artist Peter Paul Rubens to get away with 'mixing allegorical figures with representations of real personages' because 'it was his style' (*Discourse 1776*). Curiously, Johnson too, is able to mix skilfully real and allegorical figures and to enhance the universal nature of the conveyed message.

When William Hogarth was first introduced to Johnson he took him for an 'idiot' because of his odd behavioural tics but after hearing him speak he realised that Johnson could be deeply inspired. In fact, the two men shared common grounds. Hogarth could sympathise with Johnson, fully aware of the difficulties he would have experienced during the nine years he was compiling the *Dictionary* (1746-55). Hogarth's own father was a Latin teacher whose failed attempt to publish a dictionary had left the family in the debtors' prison, so at an early age Hogarth had his first experience of harsh life in prison which later engaged his artistic attention in his moral paintings and prints. Equally, Johnson admired Hogarth's *Analysis of Beauty* (1753) in which he proposed six principles of beauty, with his sinuous line of beauty, gracefully flowing yet inherently enigmatic. Further, Johnson and Hogarth sat on a committee dealing with the social issue of prostitution at the Society of Arts and both were supportive of the establishment of the Magdalen Hospital, a charitable institution for abandoned young women. Notably, Hogarth's most celebrated portrait of the orphan turned benefactor *Captain Thomas Coram* (1740) is full of allegorical objects alluding to Coram's financial success at sea; further, the Royal Charter scroll and seal granted for the establishment of the Foundling Hospital aimed to highlight Coram's generous service to society. Equally, Johnson stressed the importance of the generous efforts of the individual for the benefit of society; and that is an essential feature of his social credo as a writer.

Despite prevailing critical opinion that Johnson had no interest in the arts, recorded incidents in his correspondence confirm the contrary. There is evidence that he helped promote the 1760 exhibition at the Society of Arts and frequented exhibitions until the end of his life. For example, on 1 May he wrote to his friend Hester Thrale (1740-1821): 'The exhibition is eminently splendid. There is contour and keeping and grace and expression, all the varieties'. And in a later letter to Hester he mentioned proudly how he had run up the stairs of Somerset House to see the pictures without catching his breath. More than that, Johnson recognised the existing affinity between painting and poetry and compared them explicitly in his *Idler* No. 34 (1758) as,

> 'two arts which pursue the same end, by the operation of the same mental faculties, and which differ only as the one represents things by marks permanent and natural, the other by signs accidental and arbitrary. The one, therefore, is more easily and generally understood ... the other is capable of conveying more ideas'.

Here Johnson recognises the hidden potentials of text as an art form that is charged with more complex and conceptual meaning when compared with that of painting which strikes with the immediacy of its openly recognisable message. Art historians as disparate as Erwin Panofsky (1892-1968) and Roland Barthes (1915-80) have often queried this reductive view of mark making. Nonetheless, historical evidence confirms that painting and drawing have always had symbolic and thus culturally specific elements, and that artists followed various artistic conventions to represent feeling, movement and perspective and those have evolved in different artistic traditions. These are seen in the *Isenheim Altarpiece*, 1512-16 by Matthias Grünewald (c1470-1528), the *Martyrdom of St Sebastian*, 1473-5 by Antonio Pollaiuolo (1431/2-1498) and a *Pastoral Landscape: The Roman Campagna*, c.1639 by Claude Lorrain (1604/5-1682). It can be argued that text reduces possible interpretations while visual representation allows for a wider personal response. So for text to be akin to painting it needs to be more visually attractive; that is what Johnson stipulated and he would have aimed to achieve in his writings. Indeed, in order to charge his texts visually, Johnson needed to choose the words carefully, and it is no coincidence that his artful literary sketch of *The Vision of Theodore* and his essays for *The Rambler* were written in the middle of his epic work on the *Dictionary* between 1746 and 1755. The considerable research and discipline that went into its compilation were relieved by his musings on life, hope, wit, learning and criticism that he allowed himself in the *Rambler* essays. His *Dictionary* entries listed several meanings or uses for each word and showed how meanings varied from the most 'primitive' to the most 'philosophical'. This proved an enriching experience for Johnson that let him exploit the kindred senses of words to produce a rich multi-layered vision with parallels in the art of painting and drawing.

The Meaning of Allegory

The six *Rambler* essays and *The Vision of Theodore* are full of allegory. Johnson's *Dictionary* defined 'allegory' as 'a figurative discourse in which something other is intended than is contained in the words literally taken'. Billy Collins' poem about *The Death of Allegory* (1990) provides a contemporary reminder of familiar allegorical forms:

> I am wondering what became of all those tall abstractions
> that used to pose, robed and statuesque, in paintings
> and parade about on the pages of the Renaissance
> displaying their capital letters like license plates.
>
> Truth cantering on a powerful horse,
> Chastity, eyes downcast, fluttering with veils.
> Each one was marble come to life, a thought in a coat,
> Courtesy bowing with one hand always extended,
> …
> Even if you called them back, there are no places left
> For them to go, no Garden of Mirth or Bower of Bliss.
> The Valley of Forgiveness is lined with condominiums
> And chain saws are howling in the Forest of Despair.

The poem is cited in Gary Johnson's *The Vitality of Allegory: Figural Narrative in Modern and Contemporary Fiction* (2012) as he sets out to prove that allegory is alive and well in the twentieth and twenty-first centuries, though possibly mutating. Two hundred and fifty years ago, Johnson was able to invigorate this classical form of rhetoric and his allegorical figures in *The Rambler* may be reminiscent of John Bunyan's *The Pilgrim's Progress* (1678), but they also have striking imagery that is universal and equally apt to the sensibilities of Johnson's times. More than that, references to some social issues and scientific discoveries have modern resonance.

To be able to appreciate art, be it a text or a painting, involves a process that requires a reconstruction of the author's intention and familiarity with historical context. Indeed, an understanding of Johnson's essays by the contemporary reader can be complicated by a lack of sufficient knowledge of the period which can obscure both the original meaning and our appreciation of

Johnson's artistic skill as a writer. In the visual arts this is probably less of a problem as the reception of the work is equally as valid as the artist's intention. However, to enjoy the essays in their full richness, it is advantageous to have some guidance and Stefka's interpretive tools and Ana's illustrations provide helpful auxiliary background.

The *Rambler* Illustrations

The selected essays have been sensitively illustrated by Ana Stefanova in a way that provides both a visual summary of the dense narrative and adds a unique psychological interpretation. Ana's response shows that she has unpacked Johnson's layers of meaning and has added modern and personal connotations of her own. The illustrations can also be enjoyed for themselves, in their many styles, references, expressive colour, and playful or dark moods. Svetlan's striking photomontages capture the enduring universal aspects.

The beauty of Ana's story-telling lies in the apparent simplicity of her figures which disguise a more complex reading. Her folkloric dream-like figures inhabit a darker landscape above which they are able to float (Il. 37 In the cradle of the Night P.83), referencing Marc Chagall. The illustrations have a wit (Il. 38 The Morning is still to come P.84) and a humanity (Il. 33 Obidah on the Hills P.79) all of their own.

When Reynolds asked Johnson why he had called the magazine *The Rambler,* he explained that it was the best that had occurred to him. Johnson never gave a more definitive answer but he mentioned 'musings' and many of the essays use an introduction where he uses the workings of the mind, as the writer falls into a reverie or dream: 'I was musing on this strange inclination [Hope] ... when, falling asleep ...' (*Rambler* No. 67); 'the perusal of this passage [Life is a Voyage] having incited in me a train of reflections ... I sunk into a slumber amidst my meditations' (*Rambler* No. 102).

Svetlan Stefanov, in his artful photomontage, captures this dream-like state which can have terrifying consequences when the author is roused with a horrifying shriek (Il. 48 The Awakening from a Nightmare P.102) that is reminiscent of Edvard Munch (*The Scream*, 1893). Similarly Ana has given a psychological interpretation to the terror of despair (Il. 73 Indolence and Despair P.150).

Further, Johnson was fascinated by the inventions and discoveries of his age and wanted to educate but also to entertain in his works. In his allegorical essays he can hide all kinds of encounters for the eager reader to discover which Ana explores with an underwater bell jar and western and eastern hemispheres showing the mysteries of attempting to calculate longitude (Il. 45 Science P.97). Ana's beautiful botanical paintings (Il. 8 The destructive Force of the Poppies P.41) connote the credit given to Johnson by Erasmus Darwin for his advice in his translation of Linnaeus' *The System of Vegetables* (1783) that confirms Johnson's interest in botany. The colour and form of Ana's illustrations are outstanding. The distinctive *taches* or square brush marks in Hope (Il. 42 P.93), and sublime mountain (Il. 60 The rocks of Tenerife P.130) are surely tributes to

Paul Cézanne while the dreadful whirlpool (Il. 53 In the course of the Voyage of Life P.110) has all the spiralling energy of Vincent van Gogh. My connotations as an art historian and art lover add to my appreciation of Ana's creativity and uniqueness.

Conclusion

Literature and art share the problem of authorial intention, especially when encountered after the period in which they were created. Johnson, particularly in the *Rambler* essays, was speaking to a universal audience, using clear personifications of Wit and Wisdom; he was also introducing contemporary issues such as the bell jar and longitude, which served a didactic purpose, and despite the time lapse they would be familiar to today's readers.

Other references may no longer be recognisable and our understanding will be facilitated by Stefka's notes which focus on the multi-layered nature of the essays. As pictorial aspects of landscape and people are recognisable to a wide audience, the artistic conventions of perspective, expression and pose are indicative of certain feelings or actions that may be more culturally specific.

Further, the feelings suggested by colours, texture, form, and light and shade may connote different individual responses that depend on our personal backgrounds, knowledge and prior exposure, something that Johnson would have encouraged.

Thus, to be appreciated, his essays require active reading that can be a unique creative experience.

Peculiarities of mid-eighteenth-century Art.
Seven Interpretive Tools by Stefka Ritchie.

A. The impact of science on artistic imagination.

This Project is original in that it takes into account an important aspect of the mid-eighteenth century art and literature - that of the impact of science when reading a selection of Samuel Johnson's essays in the *Rambler*. First, it is the influence of the investigative technique of Sir Francis Bacon (1561-1626) in the advancement of knowledge as the most promising method of improving humanity's lot. But to Bacon's conceived idea of experimental science as a collaborative enterprise, guided by a strictly laid out procedure, is added the impact of the achievements of Sir Isaac Newton (1623-1727), a solitary scholar whose knowledge and intuition had contributed to the formulation of the universal laws of nature. Newton's revolutionary ideas of colour and light and matter in motion appealed to the creative impulse of the mid-eighteenth-century artistic imagination and that of Johnson.

In *Adventurer* 131 (February 5 1754) Johnson wrote:

> Whoever, after the example of Plutarch, should compare the lives of illustrious men, might set this part of Newton's character to view with great advantage, by opposing it to that of Bacon, perhaps the only man of later ages, who has any pretensions to dispute with him the palm of genius of science.

Although Johnson never came to write the parallel lives of Bacon and Newton in the fashion of Plutarch's *Lives* as he might have intended, he often recognized their influence upon his own outlook. Scholarly research is reluctant to explore the historical significance of Bacon and Newton on mid-eighteenth-century art, but it is Johnson who insisted that in order to evaluate the history of mankind and that of individuals one would have to look attentively at the peculiar character of each age. Indeed, when he appeals to the judgement of his readers, be it as a poet, writer of periodical essays and dedications, book reviewer or lexicographer, he is invoking common principles and shared expectations.

Thus, in order to grasp the essence and richness of Johnson's thinking and artistic imagination which is often undervalued, we need to become aware of the importance he places upon the existing tension between two influential traditions in the mid-eighteenth century that had lasting impact on all aspects of life. First, his respect for the empirical fact inclined him toward a similar view to Bacon who argued for truthful representation of facts, with emphasis on the practical value of knowledge rather than solely on bookish subservience to established authors. But to this has to be added the impact of Newton's revolutionary ideas of matter in motion (the *Principia* 1687) and colour and light (the *Opticks* (1704) that appealed to the artistic imagination. Newton's vision of the universe - general yet diverse and frequently diffused is often woven into the texture of the period literature and that of Johnson. Indeed, writings in the first three quarters of the eighteenth century highlight the importance it was given to imagination in the creative process. Joseph Addison's essays titled 'The pleasures of the imagination' were published in the *Spectator* (1712) and became influential in art discourse. 'Colours paint themselves on the fancy, with very little attention of thought or application of mind in the beholder. We are struck, we know not how, with the symmetry of anything we see, and immediately assent to the beauty of an object, without inquiring into the particular causes and occasions of it'. Addison noted the importance of the sense of sight as a primary vehicle in the creative process and its ability to drive the imagination by stimulating the mind to recreate images by the association of ideas.

This Project considers that there needs to be given recognition to the closeness between art and science at the time and the impact of Newtonian science on mid-eighteenth-century aesthetics. In the first quarter of the eighteenth century and particularly in the years after Newton's death in 1727, Newton had become the symbol of new science which gave birth to the greatest English scientific poetry in the century. English poets such as John Donne (1572-1631) and Thomas Browne (1605-1682) may have decried the blow suffered by the new philosophy of Copernicus which called all into doubt, and felt confused by the discoveries of comets and new stars that wandered round the Moon and Sun, and made the Earth seem small. For Donne and Browne the orderly world of Aristotle and Ptolemy had gone forever. At the time of Johnson's death in 1784, Newton may have become increasingly associated with mechanistic science, but for earlier eighteenth-century poets such as David Mallet (1705-1765), Richard Savage (1697-1743) James Thomson (1700-1748) and Edward Young (1683-1765) the Newtonian laws of nature, at once simple and diverse, had a form of flesh and blood and served to reinforce the role of imagination that was fired by the originality of Newton's vision. Propelled by exceptional sparkles of intuitive creativity, in his type of scientific approach Newton had debunked the stringency of careful planning and exploded strict experimental observation. Starting his work on planetary motion by an analogy which acted as a lever trying to open the door of a second kind of explanation and by extending Galileo's law of falling bodies to extraterrestrial motions, Newton was able to reduce one set of phenomena to another. To the perceptional sight and cognitive organization, he had added a high degree of abstraction which required tremendous ingenuity – that of 'seeing that' in the 'mind's eye'.

In *Insights of Genius* (1996), the historian of science Arthur Miller draws on his knowledge of physics to explore the nature of human creativity in the sciences, its relation to aesthetic impulses and the role of visual modelling at the interfaces of art and sciences. Miller pays particular attention to 'intuition', this sudden burst of creative thinking in which innovative ideas often emerge not in any real time sequence but in an explosion of thought and patternless data that then assumes a highly symmetrical and meaningful form. This confirms that science, as a human construction, often shares the traits of the human intellect, and this John Locke, a close friend of Newton explained in his *Essay Concerning Human Understanding* (1690) which was a philosophical interpretation of Newton's scientific thought process and which became influential in the early part of the eighteenth century.

That Johnson had a high opinion of Newton and Locke is evident from his *Rambler* writings in which he referred to them. He admired the singularity of Newton's creative process in which 'intuition' forms an integral part. In the *Dictionary* (1755) 'intuition' is defined as a 'mental vision' that is formed 'without the intervention of reason'; that 'immediate knowledge which is instantaneously accompanying the ideas which are its object'. In *Rambler* 154, Johnson likens the phenomenon of intuition to 'an unexpected flash of instruction struck out by the fortuitous collision of happy incidents'. The creative process is perceived by him as 'an involuntary concurrence of ideas, in which the philosopher to whom they happened had no other merit than that of knowing their value'. On occasions, Johnson resorted to this creative process in his own works. One may remember the moment when, during his tour of the Highlands with James Boswell in 1773, travelling between Anoth and Auchnasheal, they dismounted in a narrow valley – the very place where Johnson conceived the initial idea of the *Journey*. This is his recollection of it: 'I sat down on a bank, such as a writer of Romance might have delighted to feign', and continued to reminisce:

> I had indeed no trees to whisper over my head,
> but a clear rivulet streamed at my feet. The day was calm,
> the air soft, and all was rudeness, silence, and solitude.

The traveller's vision of the external world is restricted by 'the high hills' which hinder the eye from ranging, 'forcing the mind to find entertainment for itself'. There is something unequivocally awesome in the explicit serenity and solitude of the rugged beauty of Nature that helps the mind to turn itself in. 'Whether I spent the hour well I know not; for here I first conceived the thought of this narration', reflects Johnson, setting the tone for his diary. The final result is a mental vision in which the empirical record of facts is often interrupted by discursive reflections.

There are many instances which can confirm that art is perceived by Johnson as a variable of the imagination by the power of which the true artist recreates abstracts from experienced reality, and this Project aims to highlight the importance he placed on the pleasures of imagination in the creative process. As Johnson said to his friend Bennet Langton in a letter dated 27 June 1758: 'I know not anything more pleasant or more instructive than to compare experience with expectation'; in this way acknowledging the tension between 'Idea and Reality' and its hidden potential for art.

The selected seven pieces here confirm the skill with which Johnson recreates artistically experienced reality with tremendous imaginative power.

Peculiarities of mid-eighteenth-century Art.
Seven Interpretive Tools by Stefka Ritchie.

B. Interpretative tools

Here are seven essential interpretive tools which, though not exhaustive, should provide sufficient preparatory ammunition to help the reader to both decipher better the meaning in the selected collection of Johnson's essays (written in the mid-eighteenth century) and appreciate the artistry he applies to their execution.

(1) Looking at the 'whole', rather than solely at its parts, remains significant to mid-eighteenth-century thought, and Johnson is no exception to it. The allotted space does not permit for much elaboration on this issue but the peculiarity of this stand is linked with science, in particular, Newtonian science, which came to dominate the critical outlook particularly after his death in 1728. Newton's universal laws of Nature had pointed to a universal common thread that linked seemingly dissimilar parts into a 'whole'. Consequently, his synthesis of science had a profound influence on political ideology as a whole in the eighteenth century, cultural practices and the arts. Indeed, the shift in art from the extremely figurative and embellished to the increasingly abstract intellectual in the mid-eighteenth century coincides with the increased abstraction of Newtonian physics – that is the emphasis on the creative thinking of the mind and the importance of intuition to the perception of the 'whole' at a glance. In *Lives of the Poets* Johnson praises James Thomson's *Seasons* where the poet looks in Newtonian fashion on Nature and Life 'with a mind that at once comprehends the vast, and attends to the minute'. There in the mind's eye, on the huge poetic canvas appear the bold abstract strokes of Nature's bounties that 'swarm with life'. With unquenched thirst for knowledge, Thomson stands in awe of the infinitude of Nature, and lets his searching eye behold the astonishing view of living clouds on infinite wings. It is the same Nature that had laid open to Newton 'her latent glory', revealing a new revolutionary set of basic ideas in relation to our perception of it. It was a transformation of existing ideas and an extension or alteration of the ideas of Ptolemy, Copernicus, Galileo, Kepler and Descartes – but of such a kind that its progenitor would not have recognized it in its new form. Not surprisingly, Johnson admired also Richard Savage's poetic ability in the *Wanderer* to portray scenery in the mind's eye that was bursting with life, from the infinitely grand to the infinitely small. It was a vision much more diffused and uncertain, yet held in one whole. Johnson too would apply this approach of creating a vision in the mind's eye in pursuit of a moral tale and let the personified figures of Wit and Learning travel to the realm of Jupiter in the vast realm of the universe in *Rambler* 22 and in *Rambler* 33 Labour will journey over the Earth teaching people skills to help them improve their lives.

(2) An influential factor that helped Johnson sharpen his awareness of the 'kindred senses of words' and proved formidable in his making of a writer is the writing of the *Dictionary*. In the 'Preface to the Dictionary' he sums up the enormity of his undertaking and refers to the 'boundless variety' of illustrative quotations he had come across by saying that he had 'extracted from

philosophers principles of science; from historians remarkable facts; from chymists complete processes; from divines striking exhortations; and from poets beautiful descriptions'. As he strove to provide 'a correct standard of meaning and usage of words', Johnson became particularly aware of the delineated multiple meaning of words, from their 'primitive and natural use' to the more subtle and metaphorical ones. Here is what he says further about it:

> In every word of extensive use, it was requisite to mark the progress of its meaning, and show by what gradations of intermediate sense it has passed from its primitive to its remote and accidental signification.

In this way, 'kindred senses may be so interwoven, that the perplexity cannot be disentangled, not any reason be assigned why one should be ranged before the other', and then again, 'shades of meaning sometimes pass imperceptibly into each other, so that though on one side they apparently differ, yet it is impossible to mark the point of contact' (*Preface*, p. 31). Thus, Johnson's dexterity in usage of words needs to be taken into account when trying to uncover the multi-layered meaning of the texts.

(3) A further important dimension of Johnson's outlook is his insistence on cross-communication in the popularization of knowledge against the narrow confinement of separate disciplines. In *Rambler* 121 he recommends that 'those in possession of inexhaustible diversity of intellectual interests, kindled by the inexhaustible variety of the physical phenomena, should endeavour constantly to approach towards the inclinations of each other, thus able to fan every spark of kindred curiosity'. Johnson's diversity of interests form the essence of his general outlook in which the study of no subject is to be ignored, be it that of botany, physics, chemistry and mathematics or the arts. As an understanding of them supplied him with useful material for the popularization of knowledge – theoretical and practical which he was keen to promote as a writer, Johnson took keen interest in all of them. Thus, it should be of no surprise to today's reader that he applied the principles of science into his discourse on every day topics.

A fact to be born in mind is that Johnson lived at a time when the various disciplines were much more closely connected than they are today. And as an understanding of them supplied him with useful material for the popularization of knowledge – theoretical and practical which he was keen to promote as a writer, Johnson took interest in all of them. Here are a couple of examples to illustrate it:

In *Rambler* 101 he borrows lexis from the field of chemistry to describe the state of his own imagination in saying: 'Thus, in a short time, I had heated my imagination to such a state of activity and ebullition, that upon every occasion it fumed away in bursts of wit, and evaporations of gayety'. He energizes the imagery with the dynamism of a boiling caldron in an alchemist's laboratory. In *Rambler* 167 elements of science are again skilfully integrated into the current of general thought, revealing the boundless energy of Johnson's imagination as well as the versatility of his interests: 'Our thoughts, like rivulets issuing from distant springs, are each impregnated in its course with various mixtures, and tinged by infusions unknown to the other, yet at last easily unite into one stream'. The stress here is on variety, diverse in its singular parts, yet converging into one whole.

(4) It is apparent that science then was part of the mode of general thinking and travelled with ease by analogy across to philosophy, theology, physiology, history, the arts and numerous other unrelated disciplines. In the *Dictionary* 'art' and 'science' are interchangeable, with 'science' being 'one of the seven liberal arts, grammar, rhetorick, logick, arithmetick, musick, geometry, astronomy'. Thus, it is as plausible to suggest that whilst selecting illustrative quotations for the *Dictionary*, Johnson would have studied the effects of science over the literary mode of expression, and learned how to transform scientific notions into a new set of literary ideas.

Today, due to the advancement of the various disciplines of science, its fragmentation into separate areas of research has reached irreversible proportions. Consequently, science is often perceived by the lay person as too analytical, thus unimaginative and detached from the mode of everyday life. The fact remains that this fundamental difference of viewing science then and today might explain in a way our failure to grasp the magnitude of the imaginative power and metaphorical symbolism of scientific imagery employed by Johnson who, excited by the boldness and imaginative sweep of many scientific hypotheses of the time, was attracted by the dynamics of the scientific metaphorical expression. The specialized vocabulary of any science discipline, be it physics, botany, chemistry, or any other, was often ancillary to his ingenious application of it. This is because the writer, for Johnson, was primarily a man of wisdom who had lived and looked upon life and amassed learning from both the pages of his predecessors and from engaging directly with life, and only then was ready to teach.

(5) The task of the writer as instructor, as a person of knowledge is the fifth important tool from the list of seven. Here is Johnson's credo as a writer as formulated in *Dissertation upon poetry* in his Eastern tale and only novel *Rasselas* (1759):

> The task of the present writers is very different as it requires together
> with that learning which is to be gained from books, that experience
> which can never be attained by solitary diligence, but must arise from
> general converse, and accurate observation of the living world.

Through the literary figure of Imlac, allegedly an Eastern philosopher, Johnson lays down his rules of writing in that the first qualification of a writer should be perfect knowledge of the subject; second, knowledge has to be presented in a pleasurable way so that 'the poet who knows most, will have the power of diversifying his scenes and of gratifying the reader with remote allusions and unexpected instructions'. It is a creative approach that lends itself to visual representation – it is an approach that Johnson often applied in his writings.

(6) The way in which the description lends itself to visual representation suggesting a close link between literature and painting needs to be stressed. A prominent feature of mid-eighteenth century art, the affinity between literature and painting is well expressed by Johnson in *Idler* 34:

> Of the two parallels which have been drawn by wit and curiosity, some are literal and real, as between poetry and painting; two arts which pursue the same end, by the operation of the same mental faculties and which differ only as the one represents things by marks permanent and material, the other by signs accidental and arbitrary.

The statement is a clear indication of Johnson's acknowledgement of the closeness of writing and painting; and he goes further to clarify his point in that:

> The one therefore is more easily and generally understood, since similitude of form is immediately perceived, the other is capable of conveying more ideas, for men have thought and spoken of many things which they do not see.

And if 'words are images of things', as Johnson succinctly puts it, then it is true to say that he is well aware of the visual artistic potential of the written word, and uses it imaginatively.

(7) To encode in language the mental picture of reality and account for the reader's experience of it, Johnson uses different literary devices, one of them is Personification. It is a literary tool that heightens the reader's interest, facilitates the understanding and encourages a creative reconstruction of it. These non-human figures bear universal inherent human attributes such as envy, greed, want, desire and age which travel well across time and are as relevant today as they would have been two hundred and fifty years ago.

Others are representations of abstract ideas which may be time-bound and their meaning can prove difficult to decipher without some advance knowledge of the sensibilities of the age they come to signify. However, they always represent human traits and human values. For him Milton's *Paradise Lost* was an epic poem that was second only to Homer's *Odyssey*; nonetheless, 'The plan of *Paradise Lost* has this inconvenience, that it comprises neither human actions nor human manners' he observed; and further noted that 'the man and woman who act and suffer are in a state which no other man or woman can ever know. The reader finds no transaction in which he can be engaged, beholds no condition in which he can by any effort of imagination place himself; he has, therefore, little natural curiosity or sympathy'.

Johnson's critical comments are significant as they highlight the importance he placed on the need of the writer to engage with ordinary life that ordinary people could relate to. Thus, striving for improvement of human life his personifications embody shared human traits, qualities and ideas that are not detached from reality.

In brief, this distinct feature of the affinity between literature and art in the mid-eighteenth century and certain peculiarities of the period has led our Project team to consider having Johnson's selected essays annotated and illustrated, the latter imaginatively carried out by Ana and Svetlan.

THE RAMBLER
No 3. Tuesday, 27 March 1750

Frontispiece, The Gentleman's Magazine, Vol. XX (1750)

THE RAMBLER
No 3. Tuesday, 27 March 1750

An Allegory on Criticism

Brief Analytical Notes

Rambler 3 (Tuesday, 27 March 1750) is written in the seemingly light style of an allegory where Johnson explores the possibility, or better say the impossibility, of truthfully impartial earthly critical judgment. For the purpose of our better understanding of it, it would be helpful to remind ourselves of Johnson's own approach to criticism as he outlines it clearly in some of his other *Rambler* essays.

Johnson's critical perspective

From his early periodical essays in the *Rambler, Adventurer* and the *Idler* in the 1750s to the *Lives of the Poets* (1779-81) some decades later, Johnson's view on the nature of criticism remains the same. He believes that criticism is imperfect as it is subjected to the fallibility of human nature. In *Rambler* 93 he defines it as 'a study by which men grow important and formidable at a very small expense'. It is evident that critics, as part of the human race, share the fallibility of human nature. In the light of this, Johnson is not too surprised that the influential seventeenth-century poet John Dryden (1631-1700), for example, 'was known to have written most of his critical dissertation only to recommend the work upon which he then happened to be employed' (*Rambler* 93). The author of the *Spectator* Joseph Addison (1672-1719) too, may have rejected 'the expediency of poetical justice, because his own Cato was condemned to perish in a good cause' ('Life of Cowley'); further the author of the *Dunciad* (Alexander Pope, 1688-1744) 'places himself uncalled before the tribunal of Criticism, and solicits fame at the hazard of disgrace' ('Life of Pope'). Thus, critics in their own right are only satellites of the authors whose own judgment – a human product, is marred by partiality of opinion. Johnson is resigned to the inevitability of the subjective slant of critical bias and resolves that 'criticks, like all the rest of mankind, are very frequently misled by interest'. Further, Johnson notes that criticism has another weakness stemming from the inability of humans to comprehend 'but a very small part'; consequently instead of grasping the whole, each critic is likely to compare with a different criterion and each one to be 'referring it to a different purpose' which can lead to a discord and a lack of unanimity.

In *Rambler* 203 Johnson refers to 'the eye of the mind' which 'like that of the body, can only extend its view to new objects by losing sight of those which are now before it'. In this way, we are likely to fix our eyes upon different scenes, dividing each of them into various paths; but in moving forward, we may find ourselves even at a greater distance from each other in reaching consensus. Does this imply that there can never be absolute unanimity in critical opinion? Johnson's reply is determinedly 'no'. Because we, as 'finite beings' are 'furnished with different kinds of knowledge, exerting different degrees of attention'. This suggests that as one 'is discovering consequences which escape another', none can take in 'the whole concatenation of causes and effects'. In this way, 'of the extensive and complicated objects, parts are selected by different eyes' and since 'our minds are variously affected, as they vary our attention', there can never be unanimity of judgment (*Idler* 5). This is an accepted fact as it is mainly due to the inherent peculiarities of human nature.

The Newtonian mode of thought had shown that in questions 'diffused and compounded', it is impossible to reach unanimity of agreement because as they extend to a greater number of relations, they are likely to become more complicated and involved. And if this should be the case, in *Adventurer* 107 Johnson asks a legitimate question that has Newton's vision at heart, at once precise, universal yet somewhat enigmatic: 'Where, then is the wonder, that they, who see only a small part, should judge erroneously of the whole? Or that they, who see different and dissimilar parts, should judge differently from each other?'

An important point to be made here is that Johnson's critical outlook is influenced by the mid-eighteenth- century shift in art from the extremely figurative and embellished to the increasingly expressive which may be impacted by the increased abstraction of Newtonian physics from the world of sense perceptions, where the creativity of the mind, intuition, and perceiving of the 'whole' at a glance are central. It needs to be acknowledged that this is an outlook also favoured by Johnson. For example, in *Rambler* 176 he distinguishes two types of critics who resort to two different viewpoints. He is critical of those who read 'with the microscope of criticism' and whose attention is inevitably directed to the minutest of details that is 'scarcely visible to common observation'. In his opinion, as they discern with great exactness, they comprehend but a narrow compass and miss the general design, failing to understand how that small proportion which they are busy contemplating 'bears to the whole'. And there are the other kinds of critics who view literary works 'with the telescope of criticism'. Looking far into the distance, they miss what is immediately in front of them and are inclined to see 'some secret meaning, some remote allusion, some artful allegory, or some occult imitation which no other reader ever suspected'. In this way, caught up in a mire of triviality, they remain totally unaware of 'the cogency of argument', and are able to grasp neither 'the force of sentiment' nor 'the flowery embellishment of fancy' as the author had intended. The chosen metaphors of microscope and telescope are not coincidental as it was those new appliances that were bringing exciting new scientific discoveries in the field of physics, astronomy, biology and zoology.

Indeed, since theories are very much conditioned by the imagery available to them through language, metaphors in this sense function like analogies and can also be seen as an essential part of scientific creativity. More than that, Johnson's selected allusions to 'microscope' and 'telescope' are a deliberate choice on his part which demonstrates his skill to advance his critical point by conceptualizing one domain of entities in terms of another. In addition, the chosen metaphors involve reasoning which rests on visual imagery that incites the imagination in an act of creativity.

Despite its inherent flaws Johnson believes that criticism still has a useful role to play. For him, the rules of critical perspective are 'the instruments of mental vision', and if they are properly used, they could assist our faculties; but they could 'produce confusion and obscurity' by unskilful application. Thus, for progress to be made in the field of critical discourse as indeed in any other field, Johnson insists that pure and applied science must walk hand in hand in Baconian fashion, with examples of 'collected instances':

> Critical remarks are not easily understood without examples,
> And I have therefore collected instances of the modes of writing
> By which this species of poets, for poets they were called by
> Themselves and their admirers, was eminently distinguished
> ('Life of Cowley')

Time and time again in his writings and in real life Johnson distances himself from 'moralists' who 'instead of casting their eyes abroad in the living world, and endeavouring to form maxims of practice and new hints of theory, content their curiosity with that secondary knowledge which books afford' (*Rambler* 129). For an answer to the question of how we extract rules which can accommodate the great diversity of thought, Johnson points to the 'living world'. As a true populariser of knowledge, he resorts to botany to relate his opinion of Criticism in *Rambler* 3 which abounds in ample personifications. The allegory is a good example of the way in which science (in this instance botany) and art are fused into one.

Johnson, populariser of knowledge

It needs to be said that botany was a field of science that particularly engaged the attention of the eighteenth century and the physiology of plants formed an important aspect of it. For the *Dictionary*, Johnson borrowed definitions of lexis and illustrative quotations from the works of John Ray (1627-1705), Nehemiah Grew (1641-1712), Stephen Hales (1677-1761),) Philip Miller (1691-1771) and from *The Universal Etymological Dictionary* (1721) of Nathan Bailey (1691-1741). It needs to be remembered that botany in the eighteenth century is particularly connected with the achievement of Carl von Linnaeus (1707-1778). The publication of *System Naturae* in 1735 had established a vision for the descriptive taxonomy of plants and living organisms and that also marked a period of rapid development in taxonomic knowledge in Britain. Admittedly, the description of plants and flowers are of encyclopaedic nature in Johnson's *Dictionary* (1755) and it is likely that they would have been borrowed from available sources on the subject. However, the reduced body of descriptive material relating to botanical terminology in the revised fourth edition of the *Dictionary* in 1773 suggests that botany would have engaged the lexicographer's attention but little critical consideration has been given to this.

One good reason for this could be the prevalence of the anecdotal myth. For example, Johnson's amusing reply, 'No, Sir, I am not a botanist, and should I wish to become a botanist, I must first turn myself into a reptile' to the question, 'Are you a botanist, Dr Johnson?' is well known. However, rather than defining a lack of interest in the subject as it has been generally accepted, in his reply Johnson is very likely alluding more to his short-sightedness (*Life*, vol. I). In reality Johnson was familiar with the radical discoveries of Grew, Ray and Hales relating to the physiology of plants. Thus, the anecdote, related by contemporaries of Johnson may deceive our judgment. A further and closer examination of existing evidence will show Johnson's acquaintance with the Swedish naturalist Daniel Solander (1733-1782) and Joseph Banks (1743-1820) who circumnavigated the globe with James Cook (1728-1779) on the HMS Endeavour, collecting plant specimens accounting for new genera and species. Esteemed highly by Johnson, Banks was elected to the Literary Club on 11 December 1778 and was one of the pallbearers at Johnson's funeral. Further, Erasmus Darwin does not feature in Boswell's *Life of Johnson* nor does Johnson's interest in the ingenious theory of Linnaeus on the elaborate system of plants. But it is known that Johnson visited Darwin in 1774 and breakfasted with the Thrales at his home in Lichfield, now a museum. Another overwhelming piece of evidence is Darwin's translation of Linnaeus's *The System of Vegetables*, where in the Preface he thanks 'that Master of the English tongue Dr Samuel Johnson, for his advice on the formation of the botanic language'. Desmond King-Hele refers to some fifty botanical words for their earlier recorded usages than those cited in the OED. Could it be that some of them were coined with Johnson's assistance? Clearly, there is scope for further research.

Johnson's scepter of Criticism
Johnson here shows himself as a writer who is keen to communicate knowledge in a pleasurable way. The story goes like this: 'Being soon distinguished by the celestials, for her uncommon qualities, she [Criticism], the eldest daughter of Labour and Truth, who was committed to the care of Justice at birth and brought up by her in the celestial palace of Wisdom, was appointed the governess of Fancy, and impowered to beat time to the chorus of the Muses, when they sung before the throne of Jupiter'. He pronounces his critical judgment from a standpoint high up in the dominion of Jupiter which allows him a wide and vibrant view of the whole. Engaging the readers' sense of vision and hearing, Johnson succeeds in bringing to our attention the subjective nature of Criticism that is so much akin to the imperfections of human nature. But the mythological allusions of the past are translated into accessible forms borrowed from reality, and in this way they are given a new breadth of life that incites the mid-eighteenth century mind yet travels without difficulty to modern times.

During her visit to the 'lower world', Criticism is accompanied by the Muses and carries a scepter in her right hand given to her by Justice and the Torch of Truth in her left hand, 'an un-extinguishable torch, manufactured by Labour, and lighted by Truth, of which it was the particular quality immediately to shew everything in its true form, however it might be disguised to common eyes'. There is much movement and light in the description of the scene in which Criticism consistently uses her preferred approach as a critical judge of literary works, that is:

> Whatever was brought before her, she beheld by the steady light of the torch of Truth,
> and when her examination had convinced her,
> that the laws of just writing had been observed,

> she touched it with the amaranthine end of the scepter,
> and consigned it over to immortality.

Johnson weaves the scepter with real plants and his description of it as 'tinctured with ambrosia' and 'inwreathed with golden foliage of amaranths and bays', exhibits knowledge of the observable world of botany coupled with artistic imagination. In the *Dictionary* he tells us that 'ambrosia' denotes 'the imaginary food of the gods, eminently pleasing to the smell or taste'; whereas 'ambrosial' means 'partaking of the nature or qualities of ambrosia, fragrant, delicious, delectable' and is followed by an illustrative quotation from Milton's *Paradise Lost*: 'Thus while God spoke, ambrosial fragrance fill'd/All heaven, and in the blessed spirits elect/Sense of new joy ineffable diffis'd' [sic]. To the sense of vision and hearing is added that of smell: the scepter is at once fragrant with ambrosial scent and the potency of amaranth lends itself to the artistic imagination as Johnson explains, 'in poetry sometimes is an imaginary flower, supposed according to its name, never to fade', and supports it once again with a quotation from Milton that reads: 'Immortal amaranth! A flower which once/In paradise, fast by the tree of life,/Began to bloom, but soon, for man's offence,/to heaven removed, where first it grew, there grows,/and flo'rs aloft, shading the fount of life...'. Thus, with its delicious fragrance and heavenly smell or taste, ambrosia may well have been associated with the food of the gods, and was used by Milton, Dryden and Pope in a poetical sense, but for Johnson, it is a flower with real physical presence and natural qualities.

Johnson's scepter of Criticism has also the wicked power of the bay tree and is 'incircled with cypress and poppies, dipped in the waters of oblivion'. For a bay tree, the selected quotation in the *Dictionary* is from the Bible, Psalm xxxvii, 'I have seen the wicked in great power, and spreading himself like a green bay tree'. Cypress has a Latin derivation and is denoted concisely in the following way: 'a tall strait tree, produced with great difficulty. Its fruit is of no use: its leaves are bitter, and the very smell and shade of it are dangerous. Hence the Romans looked upon it to be a fatal tree, and made use of it at funerals, and in mournful ceremonies. The wood of the cypress-tree is always green, very heavy, of a good smell, and never either rots or is worm eaten...'. Johnson travels through centuries of human history to enlighten the reader on the meaning and significance of these plants, keen to advance their knowledge and excite their curiosity. To the potency of the bay-tree and the cypress Johnson adds the hidden power of poppies. Described as a 'plant' in the first edition of the *Dictionary* (1755), and as a 'flower' in the revised fourth edition (1773), the poppy may stand allegorically for ornament and embellishment as a flower, but in the eighteenth century it was cultivated from seed for medicine particularly for the production of opium. An addiction to opium was fatal, as after the initial euphoria, the pain returned with destructive vengeance.

Similarly, in Johnson's scepter, beneath the superficial appearance of the seemingly never fading beauty of the poppies, there is something sinister in their hidden potency which can cloud the mind and hinder judgment. Those fatal properties are further enhanced by the disparaging power of the cypress, the leaves of which though evergreen are 'bitter, and the very smell and shade of it are dangerous'. Criticism 'reversed the scepter and let drops of Lethe distil from the poppies and cypress, a fatal mildew, which immediately began to waste the work away, till it was at last totally destroyed'. Consulting the *Dictionary* again, 'mildew' is described as 'a disease that happens in plants', that 'is caused by dewy moisture which fall [sic] on them'. It is a description taken from John Hill's *Essays in natural History and Philosophy, containing a series of Discoveries, by the assistance of the Microscope* (1752). The physical properties of mildew allude to 'a thick, clammy vapour' that condenses and 'with its thick, clammy substance stops the pores, and by that means prevents perspiration'. Thus, just as in nature, mildew, 'corrodes, gnaws, and spoils the plant', so does it subject erroneous literary works to total destruction in the allegory. Also, Lethe may well have been immortalized as a fictional river of oblivion by Milton; but for Johnson its physical presence is real. To 'distil' is defined in the *Dictionary* as 'to force by fire through the vessels of distillation', and conjures up the image of Mr Sober in *Idler* 31, with his small furnace 'which he employs in distillation 'to draw oils and waters, and essences and spirits' (vol. ii, pp. 97-98). To 'distil' also denotes evaporation, formulated as 'to let fall in drops' that results in a vapour that is 'anything exhalable, anything that mingles with the air'. So, the carefully selected flowers and plants allude to a scepter poisoned by grand delusions that are finally destroyed by the fungal growth of the mildew. This is also an illustrative example of Johnson's fondness for chemistry, one of the dominant sciences, particularly after the middle of the eighteenth century.

Furnished with integrity of judgment and in pursuit of truth, Criticism rejects literary pieces that have dissimilitudes between ideas and their original objects; pieces which are linked together by incongruities, false colours or inequality between words and sentiments. But does Johnson consider Criticism's criterion of Truth achievable? So far, his observations on criticism reveal the tendency of critics to pass their judgments from the narrow premise of their own critical perspective. The fact that criticism is always likely to be marred by subjective overtones is familiar to Johnson; and the idea that human judgment is corrupted by the intrinsic deficiencies in human nature carries a somewhat pessimistic note in that ultimate truth and unbiased judgment are an unachievable goal. Thus, as she withdrew from earth with her patroness Astrea, Criticism broke her scepter, and 'left Prejudice and False Taste to ravage at large as the associates of Fraud and Mischief' on Earth'. For fear of using improperly the 'scepter of Justice', Criticism, referred the cause to be considered by Time who without reference to Flattery and Malevolence, 'passes his sentence at leisure'.

Johnson, the fact finder debunks the myth created and sustained through the ages, uniting old and new knowledge by the strokes of his poetic imagination. With amaranth, the love-lies-bleeding genus of plants, and bay, the laurel tree that extended to other trees and shrubs, only the qualities of plants as species are used, drawing on the common denominator rather than on differences. The colour and light of his artistic palette allude to his distrust of the dubious qualities of Justice – smooth and embellished on the surface, but often void of reality and fraudulent in substance akin to the fallibility of human nature.

However, perceived as a whole, Johnson's scepter of criticism in *Rambler* 3 is ingenious in design. It vibrates in all its parts that allude to Newton's spectrum of colour and light and allow for a continuous variation in pictorial reconstruction to which the reader's participation is invited. It is an artistic recreation of observable reality that reflects the sensibilities of his age.

Johnson's critical approach is instilled with the spirit of candour and love of truth; but most of all, it is a critical perspective that in seeking permanent values stands outside of time and for this it has as much modern resonance as universal appeal.

Both frontispieces, the first by the eighteenth-century artist Anthony Walker (1726-1765) and featured in the *Gentleman's Magazine* (March 1750) and the second one based on a photo art montage by Svetlan Stefanov, equally endorse Johnson's firm belief in the enduring values of art, ancient and modern.

Pleasures of the Imagination   33   Samuel Johnson Illustrated

THE RAMBLER
No 3. Tuesday, 27 March 1750

VIRTUS, *repulsæ nescia sordidæ,*
Intaminatis fulget honoribus,
Nec sumit aut pouit secures
Arbitrio popularis auræ.

HORACE. Odes. III.2.17-20.

Undisappointed in designs,
With native honours virtue shines;
Nor takes up pow'r, nor lays it down,
As giddy rabbles smile or frown.

ELPHINSTON.

Prelude to Rambler No. 3,
by Svetlan Stefanov

The task of an author is, either to teach what is not known, or to recommend known truths by his manner of adorning them; either to let new light in upon the mind, and open new scenes to the prospect, or to vary the dress and situation of common objects, so as to give them fresh grace and more powerful attractions, to spread such flowers over the regions through which the intellect has already made its progress, as may tempt it to return, and take a second view of things hastily passed over, or negligently regarded.

Either of these labours is very difficult, because, that they may not be fruitless, men must not only be persuaded of their errours, but reconciled to their guide; they must not only confess their ignorance, but, what is still less pleasing, must allow that he from whom they are to learn is more knowing than themselves.

It might be imagined that such an employment was in itself sufficiently irksome and hazardous; that none would be found so malevolent as wantonly to add weight to the stone of Sisyphus; and that few endeavours would be used to obstruct those advances to reputation, which must be made at such an expense of time and thought, with so great hazard in the miscarriage, and with so little advantage from the success.

Yet there is a certain race of men, that either imagine it their duty, or make it their amusement, to hinder the reception of every work of learning or genius, who stand as sentinels in the avenues of fame, and value themselves upon giving Ignorance and Envy the first notice of a prey.

To these men, who distinguish themselves by the appellation of Criticks, it is necessary for a new author to find some means of recommendation. It is probable, that the most malignant of these persecutors might be somewhat softened, and prevailed on, for a short time, to remit their fury.

Having for this purpose considered many expedients, I find in the records of ancient times, that Argus was lulled by musick, and Cerberus quieted with a sop; and am, therefore, inclined to believe that modern criticks, who, if they have not the eyes, have the watchfulness of Argus, and can bark as loud as Cerberus, though, perhaps, they cannot bite with equal force, might be subdued by methods of the same kind. I have heard how some have been pacified with claret and a supper, and others laid asleep by the soft notes of flattery.

Though the nature of my undertaking gives me sufficient reason to dread the united attacks of this virulent generation, yet I have not hitherto persuaded myself to take any measures for flight or treaty. For I am in doubt whether they can act against me by lawful authority, and suspect that they have presumed upon a forged commission, styled themselves the ministers of Criticism, without any authentick evidence of delegation, and uttered their own determinations as the decrees of a higher judicature.

Criticism, in the palace of Wisdom

Criticism, from whom they derive their claim to decide the fate of writers, was the eldest daughter of Labour and of Truth: she was at her birth committed to the care of Justice, and brought up by her in the palace of Wisdom. Being soon distinguished by the celestials, for her uncommon qualities, she was appointed the governess of Fancy, and empowered to beat time to the chorus of the Muses, when they sung before the throne of Jupiter.

The Scepter of Criticism

When the Muses condescended to visit this lower world, they came accompanied by Criticism, to whom, upon her descent from her native regions, Justice gave a scepter, to be carried aloft in her right hand, one end of which was tinctured with ambrosia, and inwreathed with a golden foliage of amaranths and bays; the other end was encircled with cypress and poppies, and dipped in the waters of oblivion.

In her left hand she bore an unextinguishable torch, manufactured by Labour, and lighted by Truth, of which it was the particular quality immediately to shew everything in its true form, however it might be disguised to common eyes.

Whatever Art could complicate, or Folly could confound, was, upon the first gleam of the torch of Truth, exhibited in its distinct parts and original simplicity; it darted through the labyrinths of sophistry, and shewed at once all the absurdities to which they served for refuge; it pierced through the robes, which Rhetoric often sold to Falsehood, and detected the disproportion of parts, which artificial veils had been contrived to cover.

Thus furnished for the execution of her office, Criticism came down to survey the performances of those who professed themselves the votaries of the Muses.

Whatever was brought before her, she beheld by the steady light of the torch of Truth, and when her examination had convinced her that the laws of just writing had been observed, she touched it with the amaranthine end of the scepter, and consigned it over to immortality.

The Torch of Truth

But it more frequently happened, that in the works, which required her inspection, there was some imposture attempted; that false colours were laboriously laid; that some secret inequality was found between the words and sentiments, or some dissimilitude of the ideas and the original objects; that incongruities were linked together, or that some parts were of no use but to enlarge the appearance of the whole, without contributing to its beauty, solidity, or usefulness.

Criticism descends with the Muses

Wherever such discoveries were made, and they were made whenever these faults were committed, Criticism refused the touch which conferred the sanction of immortality, and, when the errours were frequent and gross, reversed the scepter, and let drops of lethe distil from the poppies and cypress, a fatal mildew, which immediately began to waste the work away, till it was at last totally destroyed.

The distorted Parts of the Whole

There were some compositions brought to the test, in which, when the strongest light was thrown upon them, their beauties and faults appeared so equally mingled, that Criticism stood with her scepter poised in her hand, in doubt whether to shed lethe, or ambrosia, upon them. These at last increased to so great a number, that she was weary of attending such doubtful claims, and, for fear of using improperly the scepter of Justice, referred the cause to be considered by Time.

The destructive Force of the Poppies

The proceedings of Time, though very dilatory, were, some few caprices excepted, conformable to Justice: and many who thought themselves secure by a short forbearance, have sunk under his scythe, as they were posting down with their volumes in triumph to futurity. It was observable that some were destroyed by little and little, and others crushed for ever by a single blow.

The action of Time

Criticism having long kept her eye fixed steadily upon Time, was at last so well satisfied with his conduct, that she withdrew from the earth with her patroness Astrea, and left Prejudice and False Taste to ravage at large as the associates of Fraud and Mischief; contenting herself thenceforth to shed her influence from afar upon some select minds, fitted for its reception by learning and by virtue.

Criticism leaves Earth. The False Torch

Before her departure she broke her scepter, of which the shivers, that formed the ambrosial end, were caught up by Flattery, and those that had been infected with the waters of lethe were, with equal haste, seized by Malevolence. The followers of Flattery, to whom she distributed her part of the scepter, neither had nor desired light, but touched indiscriminately whatever Power or Interest happened to exhibit. The companions of Malevolence were supplied by the Furies with a torch, which had this quality peculiar to infernal lustre, that its light fell only upon faults.

No light, but rather darkness visible
Serv'd only to discover sights of woe.

PARADISE LOST, I.63-64

With these fragments of authority, the slaves of Flattery and Malevolence marched out, at the command of their mistresses, to confer immortality, or condemn to oblivion. But the scepter had now lost its power; and Time passes his sentence at leisure, without any regard to their determinations.

The Time decides

THE RAMBLER
No 22. Saturday, 2 June 1750

*Frontispiece, The Gentleman's
Magazine, Vol. XVII (1747)*

THE RAMBLER
No 22. Saturday, 2 June 1750

An Allegory on Wit and Learning

Brief Analytical notes

The Johnsonian scholar James Clifford was right in saying that Johnson was one of the most skilled users of symbolic names, and *Rambler* 22 is an excellent example of the way in which Johnson adeptly integrates name devices into the theme of the essay that is rich on personifications. To build up the portraits of Wit and Learning in their eighteenth-century connotation, he uses the ancient images of Apollo, the celebrated Greek god of music, poetry and the arts, that of Euphrosyne, one of the three Greek graces representing charity and merriment, as well as Sophia, the Hellenistic goddess of wisdom together with Minerva, the Roman goddess of wisdom and sponsor of the arts. The tale is strewn with Homeric imagery enticing the eighteenth-century reader to learn more about Greek and Roman art through Greek and Roman writers. Johnson knew many of their works and his command of Latin and Greek allowed him to read them in the original.

Johnson creates the profiles of Wit and Learning against the backdrop of ancient mythological characters, and his purpose is twofold. On one hand, he wants to encourage curiosity and learning in a pleasurable way. On the other hand, he uses the ancient characters to paint a picture of his times. In *The Dictionary*, Johnson defines 'learning as Literature; skill in languages or sciences; generally scholastick knowledge' and illustrates it with a quotation from Bacon's *Essays* that reads: 'Learning hath its infancy, when it is almost childish; then its youth, when luxuriant and juvenile; then its strength of years, when solid; and, lastly, its old age, when dry and exhaust'. The original signification of Wit, on the other hand, is denoted by Johnson as 'the powers of the mind; the mental faculties; the intellects', and refers to 'imagination and quickness of fancy', and is supported with a quotation from Locke who stresses that the essence of Wit lies 'most in the assemblage of ideas, and putting those together with quickness and variety' (*The Dictionary*).

Similarly, Johnson's Wit and Learning bear those main traits; namely, that on the surface, with his cheerful and engaging manners full of frivolity and quickness of action, Wit was more attractive to the young; while Learning, eloquent but entrenched in a narrow position was ready to reject every new notion, and could only charm the older with her perplexing disputations. As a true follower of Bacon's method of induction, Johnson favoured the role of experience which in the words of Bacon, 'first lights the candle, and then by means of the candle shows the way; commencing as it does with experience duly ordered and digested, not bungling or erratic' (*Novum Organum*, Book I). In one of his striking metaphorical images Bacon compares reasoners to spiders who like scholastic dogmatists make cobwebs out of their own entrails. And for those who choose first to draw their conclusions out of a preconceived framework before they have familiarised themselves with the facts, like Learning in Johnson's fable, this is likely to prove a self-defeating exercise.

More than that, as a writer with a social agenda, by making both divinities, Wit and Learning, to be disregarded by those mortals who were devoted to Plutus, the god of riches, Johnson levies his criticism on selfish wealth. On more than one occasion in his writings he would vent his anger against society for failing its most vulnerable members such as debtors lingering in prisons, destitute orphans and young girls subjected to misery and hopelessness and forced into prostitution. As early as 1738 Johnson had described the metropolis in his poem *London* as a place where 'malice, rapine, accident, conspire', a place that remained insensitive to the misery of the most vulnerable members of society who languished in poverty. It is not surprising that he was one of the leading members of the Society for the Encouragement of Arts, Manufactures and Commerce (for short, the Society of Arts) who engaged their benevolent efforts in the establishment of the Magdalen Hospital in 1758, a reformatory for young females. It is acknowledged by social historians such as Sophie Carter, Jennie Batchelor and Mary Peace amongst others that it was Johnson who first drew public attention to the existing grave social problem of prostitution through his portrayal of destitute girls in his *Rambler* essays as early as the 1750s. Many of these writings confirm that his agenda of social improvement was deeply embedded in them (*Rambler* 107, *Rambler* 170 and 171). The progressive social agenda is restated in the moving conclusion of Misela's story which works on two levels: expository of the abhorrent living conditions of the protagonist and reformatory, that is appealing to the consciousness of the wealthy members of society to change their unsympathetic behaviour to a benevolent one; and rather than nurture their vice to show compassion by positive charitable deeds to help 'rescue such numbers of human beings from a state so dreadful'.

Further, in the present story, expelled by Jupiter to 'the lower world', the protagonists Wit and Learning ask him for re-admission to the ethereal spaces. Johnson's choice of Jupiter is not coincidental. The most powerful god in Roman mythology, Jupiter was also relevant to mid-eighteenth-century science. The royal observatories at Paris and Greenwich were regularly publishing tables of the predicted eclipses of Jupiter's satellites hoping to find the solution to the longitude problem. There is no doubt that discoveries in astronomy in the seventeenth century in general and particularly those of Newton had led to a marked tendency to popularise its study in the eighteenth century. For example, James Ferguson, FRS, whom Johnson knew personally, wrote books on scientific issues and lectured round the country from the 1760s. 'Of all the sciences cultivated by mankind, Astronomy is acknowledged to be and undoubtedly is the most sublime, the most interesting, and the most useful', conceded Ferguson, and proceeded to explain the principles of Newton's philosophy in an allegedly easy style in *Astronomy explained upon Sir Isaac Newton's Principles*. Women, too, tried to understand, in the words of Ferguson, how 'by the help of telescopes we discover thousands of Stars which are invisible to the bare eye; and the better our glasses are, still the more become visible; so that we can set no limits either to their number or their distances'. The poetess Mary Leapor who died in 1746 aged only twenty-four, timidly asked questions about the sun, moon, stars and Elizabeth Carter, a contributor to the *Gentleman's Magazine* and a friend of Johnson, made a translation of Algarotti's *Newtonianism for the Ladies*. In some of his *Rambler* essays Johnson confirms his interest in astronomy too. In *Rambler* 61 his character Ruricola compares her dissatisfaction of receiving old news with the perpetual deception of 'a man pointing his telescope at a remote star, which before the light reaches his eye has forsaken the place from which it was emitted'. In *Rambler* 91 Jupiter acts as arbiter to the complaints of the Sciences who 'put up their petition' to him 'for a more equitable distribution of richer and honours'. In this densely animated allegorical piece, Johnson weaves a challenging theme on the essential role of the sciences as independent promoters of knowledge. Critical of Patronage, he sends the Sciences on their quest for justice and after their long wander they 'were led at last to the cottage of Independence, the daughter of Fortitude, where they were taught by Prudence and Parsimony to support themselves in dignity and quiet'. These are just two examples in which Johnson subsumes concepts of astronomy for the purpose of illustration of debated ideas of general nature.

But Johnson's keen interest in the subject of astronomy is perhaps best captured on the vast canvas of *Rasselas* and his depiction of Pekuah's study of astronomy exemplifies also his positive stand on learning in general and confirms the encouragement he also gave to women in the advancement of knowledge. Initially with 'no great inclination to this study', Pekuah, princess Nekayah's maid, sought more knowledge on the subject from the Astronomer, and once she gained access to him the discourse turned to astronomy, 'he looked upon her as a prodigy of genius, and intreated [sic] her not to desist from a study which she had so happily began'. Imlac, too, recalls how during one of his visits to the turret of the Astronomer's house, while 'watching the emersion of a satellite of Jupiter', there 'a sudden tempest clouded the sky', and disappointed their observation'. It is not surprising that the room of the Astronomer gets steeped in darkness before light emerges again as it was a known fact then that, if viewed with a large telescope, Jupiter exhibited a variety of changing detail and colour in its cloudy atmosphere. There is no doubt that Johnson would have been able to gain a first-hand experience in the observation of Jupiter and the eclipses of its satellites from his young friend Topham Beauclerk's well equipped observatory in Windsor. To appreciate Johnson's artistic brushstrokes, it is necessary to understand the essence of this physical phenomenon that was engaging the attention of his contemporaries and that was linked with the longitude issue.

To show that the vigour of Wit and the perspicacity of Learning are equally important, Johnson joins them in matrimony and perpetual concord; so to speak imagination and inventiveness are added to theoretical knowledge to form a whole new creative experience, with offsprings to serve the Arts and Sciences at a time when in the advancement of knowledge art and science were feeding upon each other in an imaginative reconstruction of experienced reality in a Baconian fashion in that while particular sciences must evolve, they must not develop in isolation, but in relation to contiguous sickness with overlapping of various studies that combined physical, chemical and biological knowledge. Experiments on combustion to those on metals and minerals and the nature and properties of air, which itself has common ground with the investigation on plant growth, and on the physiological study of respiration; to the study of heat and temperature, light and sound – were all an outstanding vindication of Bacon's dictum that science should involve the study of continuous processes in action. Further, Newton had shown that at times, intuition, that most creative intellectual activity that involved metaphorical thinking, was essential for the creative process and enabled him to fuse art and science into a whole.

In brief, this seemingly simple and heavily personified story strikes with a flurry of movement through earthy and ethereal space and offers an insight into Johnson's attitude to knowledge and the arts in that knowledge of the works of predecessors does not suffice for the creative process unless it is coupled with a personal imaginative drive with virtually autistic moments of rich and often disordered aesthetic productivity where the role of visual modelling at the interface between science and art remains paramount.

THE RAMBLER
No 22. Saturday, 2 June 1750

—*Ego nec studium sine divite venû,*
Nec rude quid prosit video ingenium; alterius sic
Altera poscit opem res, et conjurat amice.

Hor. Ars. Poetica, II. 409-11.

Without a genius learning soars in vain;
And without learning genius sinks again;
Their force united crowns the sprightly reign.

Elphinston.

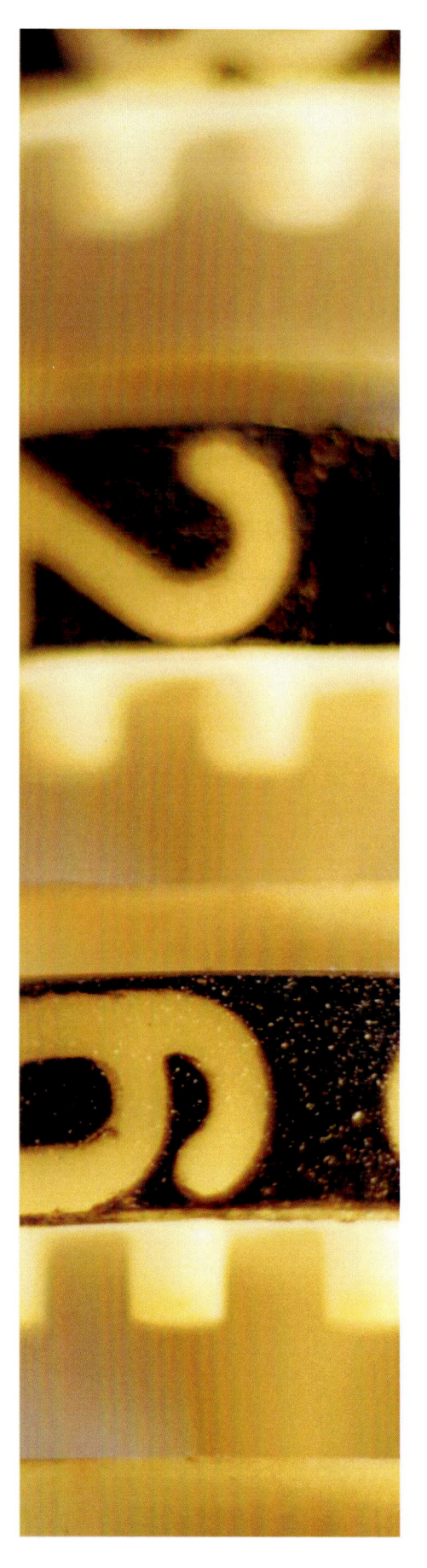

Prelude to Rambler No. 22,
by Svetlan Stefanov

Wit and Learning were the children of Apollo, by different mothers; Wit was the offspring of Euphrosyne, and resembled her in cheerfulness and vivacity; Learning was born of Sophia, and retained her seriousness and caution. As their mothers were rivals, they were bred up by them from their birth in habitual opposition, and all means were so incessantly employed to impress upon them a hatred and contempt of each other, that though Apollo, who foresaw the ill effects of their discord, endeavoured to soften them, by dividing his regard equally between them, yet his impartiality and kindness were without effect; the maternal animosity was deeply rooted, having been intermingled with their first ideas, and was confirmed every hour, as fresh opportunities occurred of exerting it. No sooner were they of age to be received into the apartments of the other celestials, than Wit began to entertain Venus at her toilet, by aping the solemnity of Learning, and Learning to divert Minerva at her loom, by exposing the blunders and ignorance of Wit.

Thus they grew up, with malice perpetually increasing, by the encouragement which each received from those whom their mothers had persuaded to patronize and support them; and longed to be admitted to the table of Jupiter, not so much for the hope of gaining honour, as of excluding a rival from all pretensions to regard, and of putting an everlasting stop to the progress of that influence which either believed the other to have obtained by mean arts and false appearances.

At last the day came, when they were both, with the usual solemnities, received into the class of superior deities, and allowed to take nectar from the hand of Hebe. But from that hour Concord lost her authority at the table of Jupiter. The rivals, animated by their new dignity, and incited by the alternate applauses of the associate powers, harassed each other by incessant contests, with such a regular vicissitude of victory, that neither was depressed.

It was observable, that, at the beginning of every debate, the advantage was on the side of Wit; and that, at the first sallies, the whole assembly sparkled, according to Homer's expression, with unextinguishable merriment. But Learning would reserve her strength till the burst of applause was over, and the languor with which the violence of joy is always succeeded, began to promise more calm and patient attention. She then attempted her defence, and, by comparing one part of her antagonist's objections with another, commonly made him confute himself; or, by shewing how small a part of the question he had taken into his view, proved that his opinion could have no weight. The audience began gradually to lay aside their prepossessions, and rose, at last, with great veneration for Learning, but with greater kindness for Wit.

Wit and Learning

Their conduct was, whenever they desired to recommend themselves to distinction, entirely opposite. Wit was daring and adventurous; Learning cautious and deliberate. Wit thought nothing reproachful but dullness; Learning was afraid of no imputation but that of error. Wit answered before he understood, lest his quickness of apprehension should be questioned; Learning paused, where there was no difficulty, lest any insidious sophism should lie undiscovered. Wit perplexed every debate by rapidity and confusion; Learning tired the hearers with endless distinctions, and prolonged the dispute without advantage, by proving that which never was denied. Wit, in hopes of shining, would venture to produce what he had not considered, and often succeeded beyond his own expectation, by following the train of a lucky thought; learning would reject every new notion, for fear of being entangled in consequences which she could not foresee, and was often hindered, by her caution, from pressing her advantages, and subduing her opponent.

Both had prejudices, which, in some degree, hindered their progress towards perfection, and left them open to attacks. Novelty was the darling of wit, and antiquity of learning. To wit, all that was new was specious; to learning, whatever was ancient was venerable. Wit, however, seldom failed to divert those whom he could not convince, and to convince was not often his ambition; learning always supported her opinion with so many collateral truths, that, when the cause was decided against her, her arguments were remembered with admiration.

Nothing was more common, on either side, than to quit their proper characters, and to hope for a complete conquest by the use of the weapons which had been employed against them. Wit would sometimes labour a syllogism, and learning distort her features with a jest; but they always suffered by the experiment, and betrayed themselves to confutation or contempt. The seriousness of wit was without dignity, and the merriment of learning without vivacity.

The rivals harass each other

Their contests, by long continuance, grew at last important, and the divinities broke into parties. Wit was taken into protection of the laughter-loving Venus, had a retinue allowed him of smiles and jests, and was often permitted to dance among the graces. Learning still continued the favourite of Minerva, and seldom went out of her palace without a train of the severer virtues, chastity, temperance, fortitude, and labour.

Wit protected by Venus and Learning, the favourite of Minerva

Wit, cohabiting with malice, had a son named satire, who followed him, carrying a quiver filled with poisoned arrows, which, where they once drew blood, could by no skill ever be extracted.

Wit, Malice and their son Satyr

These arrows he frequently shot at learning, when she was most earnestly or usefully employed, engaged in abstruse inquiries, or giving instructions to her followers. Minerva, therefore, deputed criticism to her aid, who generally broke the point of Satyr's arrows, turned them aside, or retorted them on himself.

Jupiter was at last angry that the peace of the heavenly regions should be in perpetual danger of violation, and resolved to dismiss these troublesome antagonists to the lower world. Hither, therefore, they came, and carried on their ancient quarrel among mortals, nor was either long without zealous votaries. Wit, by his gaiety, captivated the young; and Learning, by her authority, influenced the old. Their power quickly appeared by very eminent effects; theatres were built for the reception of Wit, and colleges endowed for the residence of Learning. Each party endeavoured to outdo the other in cost and magnificence, and to propagate an opinion, that it was necessary, from the first entrance into life, to enlist in one of the factions; and that none could hope for the regard of either divinity, who had once entered the temple of the rival power.

Wit and Learning amongst the Mortals

There were, indeed, a class of mortals, by whom wit and learning were equally disregarded: these were the devotees of Plutus, the god of riches; among these it seldom happened that the gaiety of Wit could raise a smile, or the eloquence of Learning procure attention. In revenge of this contempt they agreed to incite their followers against them; but the forces that were sent on those expeditions frequently betrayed their trust; and, in contempt of the orders which they had received, flattered the rich in public, while they scorned them in their hearts; and when, by this treachery, they had obtained the favour of Plutus, affected to look with an air of superiority on those who still remained in the service of Wit and Learning.

Pluto, the god of Riches

Disgusted with these desertions, the two rivals, at the same time, petitioned Jupiter for readmission to their native habitations. Jupiter thundered on the right hand, and they prepared to obey the happy summons.

Wit readily spread his wings and soared aloft, but not being able to see far, was bewildered in the pathless immensity of the ethereal spaces.

Learning, who knew the way, shook her pinions; but for want of natural vigour could only take short flights: so, after many efforts, they both sunk again to the ground, and learned, from their mutual distress, the necessity of union.

They therefore joined their hands, and renewed their flight: Learning was borne up by the vigour of Wit, and Wit guided by the perspicacity of Learning. They soon reached the dwellings of Jupiter, and were so endeared to each other, that they lived afterwards in perpetual concord. Wit persuaded Learning to converse with the Graces, and Learning engaged Wit in the service of the Virtues. They were now the favourites of all the powers of heaven, and gladdened every banquet by their presence. They soon after married, at the command of Jupiter, and had a numerous progeny of Arts and Sciences.

Wit and Learning readmitted by Jupiter

The Marriage of Wit and Learning

THE RAMBLER
No. 33. Tuesday, 10 July 1750

Frontispiece, The Gentleman's Magazine, Vol. XXI (1751)

THE RAMBLER
No. 33. Tuesday, 10 July 1750

An Allegory on Rest and Labour

Brief Analytical Notes

Mrs Hester Thrale, a good friend of Johnson since the mid 1760s said his *Rambler* 33 was Johnson's favourite. It can be said that this piece of writing is overwhelmingly conditioned by the marked shift in mid-eighteenth-century attitude to socio-economic and environmental change, and as it reveals Johnson's own interest in social issues, it needs special attention.

The allegory begins with an allusion of the prelapsarian state of man, those 'early ages of the world', when life was marked by plenty and when divisions were unknown. The description bears strong resemblance to the story of Genesis, a combination of creative and historical myth. However, Johnson gives his own interpretation of the Fall of Man by putting the main reason for it on the imperfections of human nature regardless of gender and race rather than on the alleged sin of Eve that is embedded in the Judeo-Christian tradition. The depiction of the birth of civilisation is no longer bound by the mythical dominance of any one culture which allows him to create a generic picture of 'a time of continual pleasure, and constant plenty under the protection of Rest':

> A gentle divinity, who required of her worshippers neither altars nor sacrifices, and whose rites were only performed by prostrations upon turfs of flowers in shades of jasmine and myrtle, or by dances on the banks of rivers flowing with milk and nectar.

The personification of Rest who is raised high on a pedestal of a divinity confirms the importance Johnson places on the need for relaxation in human life. The description also demonstrates his awareness of the potency of words; it reveals his skill in using them as precious brushstrokes against the backdrop of ancient times of alleged 'original integrity' in the human race. The painted prospect delights with its pastoral felicity: the abundance of delicious fruits, colourful birds and a variety of beasts conjure up an image of 'perpetual spring', free of imposed worship, be it pagan or religious. Further, this paradise lost may be reminiscent of the poetic epics of Homer and Milton amongst other prominent literary works along the lines of the human odyssey; but the international reader is not bound by any particular knowledge; for this the propagated ideas by Johnson have a universal appeal which was no doubt his intention.

However, Johnson doubts the existence of such an ideal world at any point in history in view of the prevalent corruption of human nature that often leads to 'violence and fraud, and theft and rapine'; consequently, man is faced with the harsh reality of seasonal changes and 'famine, with a thousand diseases'. With a focus on the idea of the 'fall of man' and the loss of his 'original integrity' that transcends national boundaries, attention is given to those generic traits such as violence, envy, corruption amongst others that are deeply ingrained in human nature and are the cause of inclemency, devastation and famine – all man-made historical disasters that continue to be poignant today. Notably, this paradisiacal setting also alludes to the natural rights of man – to the basic necessities of life – that became a much discussed philosophical issue during the eighteenth century under the influence of the seventeenth-century philosophies of Hugo Grotius (1583-1645), Thomas Hobbes (1588-1679) and John Locke (1632-1704). These had fundamental consequences in all spheres of life. Johnson was familiar with their ideas and on occasions referred to them in his own writings.

Further, as a writer with a social agenda, Johnson is always keen to first expose the problem and then seek a solution for it. In the *Dictionary*, 'famine n.s. [famine, French; fames, Latin.]' is described by Johnson as 'scarcity of food; dearth; distress for want of victuals'. One of the selected illustrative quotations is from Hale's *Origin of Mankind* and reads: 'Famines have not been of late observed, partly because of the industry of mankind, partly by those supplies that come by sea to countries in want, but principally by the goodness of God'. In the allegory, Johnson conveys the same sentiment through the personified figure of Labour 'the son of Necessity, the nurseling of Hope and the pupil of Art' as a vehicle for social improvement. His 'wrinkled with the wind' face is 'swarthy with the sun', bears no traces of godlike aura; nonetheless, it has awe-inspiring presence.

Equipped with the implements of husbandry in one hand and the tools of architecture in the other, Labour embraces the whole universe by offering to teach 'the inhabitants of the globe' how 'to remedy the sterility of the earth, and the severity of the sky'. As a true preceptor, Labour is ready to inform and guide humans in procuring ways of 'piercing the bowels of the earth' to extract 'from the caverns of the mountains metals' which will help them 'subject all nature' to their 'use and pleasure'. Incited by his encouragement, 'the inhabitants of the globe considered Labour as their only friend, and hasted to his command' and followed his advice on how to 'open mines, to level hills, to drain marshes, and change the course of rivers'.

There is nothing mystical in Labour's daring vision of 'land covered with towns and villages, encompassed with the fields of corn, and plantations of fruit-trees'; of land of plenty - with 'heaps of grain' and tables full of 'baskets of fruit'. In fact, this far-reaching utopian vision that is instilled with the spirit of public dedication and public good pervades the allegory and provides a context for our understanding of the relationship between mid-eighteenth-century radicalism and attitudes to human progress. In this sense, the allegory endorses Johnson's interest in social progress, and the fact that he valued highly his writing of it is a clear endorsement of it. Further, the practical slant of Labour's teaching through inventions and improvements captures the aspirations of the Society for the Encouragement of Arts, Manufactures and Commerce whose member Johnson was from 1756 to 1762. It is likely that the humanitarian ethos and activities of the Society would have drawn Johnson to become its member almost from the beginning of its foundation.

However, written in 1750, Johnson's allegory on Labour and Rest predates the formation of the Society in 1755, and highlights his firm personal stand on human progress and commitment to the betterment of human life. His writings on dire poverty, the deplorable state of prisons with putrid and unwholesome air that led often to fevers, infections and diseases, and his praise of the ventilator invented by Stephen Hales FRS (1677-1761) and installed in Newgate prison in 1752 and other public buildings confirm this.

Similarly, in the concluding part of the allegory Johnson promotes the idea that social welfare should be a balance between work and rest and he illustrates that through the close association between Labour and Rest. Their offspring Health is a personified figure of 'a benevolent goddess, who consolidated the union of her parents', and dispenses her gifts 'to those who shared their lives in just proportions between Rest and Labour'. Johnson's argument for a fine balance between work and relaxation more than two and a half centuries ago is relevant today, and this gives the allegory a strikingly contemporary slant as well as a universal appeal.

It needs to be remembered that Johnson lived in a time that fostered and channelled people's energies towards the encouragement of the acquisition of theoretical knowledge and practical skills vindicating the advantages of a commercial society, and marking the beginning of the Industrial Revolution. 'Improvement' was an increasingly pervasive theme in British discourse comprising self-improvement and public improvement. More than fifty years ago the historian Asa Briggs noted that the word 'improvement' had a long history and was 'part of the working vocabulary of Dr Johnson and Daniel Defoe' (*The Age of Improvement*, 1959). In *The Dictionary*, 'to improve' is defined by Johnson as betterment in physical terms as well as advancement in goodness. So, an 'improvement' related to material as well as moral or spiritual qualities and those two concepts went hand in hand. Indeed, browsing thorough Johnson's *Diary* it becomes evident that the pursuit of improvement aiming at the betterment of life engaged his attention, and this needs to be taken into account when discussing his profile as a person and writer as it forms part of his social morality.

As to the artistic execution of the allegory, worth noting is the way in which Johnson portrays Labour soaring up, staying aloft and gliding along over the globe, held down by gravity, as Newton had postulated in the *Principia*. It is an exhilarating avian flight that seeks to illuminate depth and vastness; likewise it allows for social and spatial relations to be explored. As various sights recede from the picture plane, they render intensity of colour and depth. In addition, the imagery alludes to the man's historical yearning for flying that occupied progressively eighteenth-century science. Indeed, consulting the timeline of aviation throughout the century confirms that hot-air ballooning was followed with excitement on the Continent; and that Johnson shared this enthusiasm throughout his life is evident from Chapter VI titled, 'A Dissertation on the Art of Flying', *Rasselas* (1759); from his acquaintance with leading pioneers in hot-air balloon flying in Britain such as Vincenzo Lunardi (1759-1806) and James Sadlers (1753-1826); and from his letters to Edmund Burke, Joshua Reynolds,

Hester Thrale, William Windham amongst others. On 29 September 1784 he wrote to Boswell, 'On one day I had three letters about air-balloon...' And in a later letter dated 6 October, Johnson expressed his doubts with admirable foresight in that 'a method of mounting into the air' of air-balloons is now known, but these 'vehicles can serve no other purpose until we learn to navigate them'. Interestingly, Richard Holmes notes the incident of the disastrous loss of Sadler's instrument during his second ascent on 12 November 1784 in *The Age of Wonder* (2008).

It is known that Johnson bequeathed to the adventurous Oxford aeronaut, the son of a lowly artisan, an enormously expensive barometer said to be worth 200 guineas to be used on future flights. This is one example of the way in which Johnson often supported the endeavours of individuals who were keen to engage in the advancement of science for the common good.

In conclusion, this allegory reveals Johnson's ability to encode pertinent eighteenth-century issues with artistic ingenuity in an entertaining way. Moreover, it outlines his social credo – a masterfully executed vision of a paradise regained through work of careful planning and scientific development balanced by purposeful rest and sound health. Grappling today with social issues connected with uneven global economic development, poverty and public health concerns, Johnson's foresight can travel universally with ease to the twenty-first century reader, bridging the centuries-long gap.

THE RAMBLER
No. 33. Tuesday, 10 July 1750

Quod caret alterna requie, durabile non est.

Ovid, Heroides, Epist. iv. 89.

Alternate rest and labour long endure.

*Prelude to Rambler No. 33,
by Svetlan Stefanov*

In the early ages of the world, as is well known to those who are versed in ancient traditions, when innocence was yet untainted, and simplicity unadulterated, mankind was happy in the enjoyment of continual pleasure, and constant plenty, under the protection of Rest; a gentle divinity, who required of her worshippers neither altars nor sacrifices, and whose rites were only performed by prostrations upon turfs of flowers in shades of jasmine and myrtle, or by dances on the banks of rivers flowing with milk and nectar.

In the early Ages

Under this easy government the first generations breathed the fragrance of perpetual spring, ate the fruits, which, without culture, fell ripe into their hands, and slept under bowers arched by nature, with the birds singing over their heads, and the beasts sporting about them. But by degrees they began to lose their original integrity; each, though there was more than enough for all, was desirous of appropriating part to himself. Then entered violence and fraud, and theft and rapine. Soon after Pride and Envy broke into the world, and brought with them a new standard of wealth; for men, who, till then, thought themselves rich when they wanted nothing, now rated their demands, not by the calls of nature, but by the plenty of others; and began to consider themselves as poor, when they beheld their own possessions exceeded by those of their neighbours. Now only one could be happy, because only one could have most, and that one was always in danger, lest the same arts by which he had supplanted others should be practised upon himself.

The Fall

Amidst the prevalence of this corruption, the state of the earth was changed; the year was divided into seasons; part of the ground became barren, and the rest yielded only berries, acorns, and herbs. The summer and autumn indeed furnished a coarse and inelegant sufficiency, but winter was without any relief: Famine, with a thousand diseases which the inclemency of the air invited into the upper regions, made havoc among men, and there appeared to be danger lest they should be destroyed before they were reformed.

To oppose the devastations of Famine, who scattered the ground everywhere with carcases, Labour came down upon earth. Labour was the son of Necessity, the nurseling of Hope, and the pupil of Art; he had the strength of his mother, the spirit of his nurse, and the dexterity of his governess. His face was wrinkled with the wind, and swarthy with the sun; he had the implements of husbandry in one hand, with which he turned up the earth; in the other he had the tools of architecture, and raised walls and towers at his pleasure. He called out with a rough voice, "Mortals! see here the power to whom you are consigned, and from whom you are to hope for all your pleasures, and all your safety. You have long languished under the dominion of Rest, an impotent and deceitful goddess, who can neither protect nor relieve you, but resigns you to the first attacks of either Famine or Disease, and suffers her shades to be invaded by every enemy, and destroyed by every accident.

Labour, the son of Necessity, the pupil of Art

"Awake therefore to the call of Labour. I will teach you to remedy the sterility of the earth, and the severity of the sky; I will compel summer to find provisions for the winter; I will force the waters to give you their fish, the air its fowls, and the forest its beasts; I will teach you to pierce the bowels of the earth, and bring out from the caverns of the mountains metals which shall give strength to your hands, and security to your bodies, by which you may be covered from the assaults of the fiercest beast, and with which you shall fell the oak, and divide rocks, and subject all nature to your use and pleasure."

Encouraged by this magnificent invitation, the inhabitants of the globe considered Labour as their only friend, and hasted to his command. He led them out to the fields and mountains, and shewed them how to open mines, to level hills, to drain marshes, and change the course of rivers. The face of things was immediately transformed; the land was covered with towns and villages, encompassed with fields of corn, and plantations of fruit-trees; and nothing was seen but heaps of grain, and baskets of fruit, full tables, and crowded storehouses.

Thus Labour and his followers added every hour new acquisitions to their conquests, and saw Famine gradually dispossessed of his dominions; till at last, amidst their jollity and triumphs, they were depressed and amazed by the approach of Lassitude, who was known by her sunk eyes and dejected countenance.

She came forward trembling and groaning: at every groan the hearts of all those that beheld her lost their courage, their nerves slackened, their hands shook, and the instruments of labour fell from their grasp.

Shocked with this horrid phantom, they reflected with regret on their easy compliance with the solicitations of Labour, and began to wish again for the golden hours which they remembered to have passed under the reign of Rest, whom they resolved again to visit, and to whom they intended to dedicate the remaining part of their lives.

Rest had not left the world; they quickly found her, and to atone for their former desertion, invited her to the enjoyment of those acquisitions which Labour had procured them.

Lassitude

Rest therefore took leave of the groves and valleys, which she had hitherto inhabited, and entered into palaces, reposed herself in alcoves, and slumbered away the winter upon beds of down, and the summer in artificial grottoes with cascades playing before her. There was indeed always something wanting to complete her felicity, and she could never lull her returning fugitives to that serenity which they knew before their engagements with Labour: nor was her dominion entirely without control, for she was obliged to share it with Luxury, though she always looked upon her as a false friend, by whom her influence was in reality destroyed, while it seemed to be promoted.

The two soft associates, however, reigned for some time without visible disagreement, till at last Luxury betrayed her charge, and let in Disease to seize upon her worshippers. Rest then flew away, and left the place to the usurpers; who employed all their arts to fortify themselves in their possession, and to strengthen the interest of each other.

Rest had not always the same enemy: in some places she escaped the incursions of Disease; but had her residence invaded by a more slow and subtle intruder, for very frequently, when everything was composed and quiet, when there was neither pain within, nor danger without, when every flower was in bloom, and every gale freighted with perfumes, Satiety would enter with a languishing and repining look, and throw herself upon the couch placed and adorned for the accommodation of Rest. No sooner was she seated than a general gloom spread itself on every side, the groves immediately lost their verdure, and their inhabitants desisted from their melody, the breeze sunk in sighs, and the flowers contracted their leaves, and shut up their odours. Nothing was seen on every side but multitudes wandering about they knew not whether, in quest they knew not of what; no voice was heard but of complaints that mentioned no pain, and murmurs that could tell of no misfortune.

Luxury lets in Disease, Satiety and Lassitude

Rest had now lost her authority. Her followers again began to treat her with contempt; some of them united themselves more closely to Luxury, who promised by her arts to drive Satiety away; and others, that were more wise, or had more fortitude, went back again to Labour, by whom they were indeed protected from Satiety, but delivered up in time to Lassitude, and forced by her to the bowers of Rest.

Thus Rest and Labour equally perceived their reign of short duration and uncertain tenure, and their empire liable to inroads from those who were alike enemies to both. They each found their subjects unfaithful, and ready to desert them upon every opportunity. Labour saw the riches which he had given always carried away as an offering to Rest, and Rest found her votaries in every exigence flying from her to beg help of Labour. They, therefore, at last determined upon an interview, in which they agreed to divide the world between them, and govern it alternately allotting the dominion of the day to one, and that of the night to the other, and promised to guard the frontiers of each other, so that, whenever hostilities were attempted, Satiety should be intercepted by Labour, and Lassitude expelled by Rest.

Health, the daughter of Labour and Rest

Thus the ancient quarrel was appeased, and as hatred is often succeeded by its contrary, Rest afterwards became pregnant by Labour, and was delivered of Health, a benevolent goddess, who consolidated the union of her parents, and contributed to the regular vicissitudes of their reign, by dispensing her gifts to those only who shared their lives in just proportions between Rest and Labour.

THE RAMBLER
No 65. Tuesday, 30 October 1750

Frontispiece, The Gentleman's Magazine, Vol. XIX (1749)

THE RAMBLER
No 65. Tuesday, 30 October 1750

Obidah and the Hermit - An Eastern Story.

Brief Analytical Notes
Rambler 65 is one of five Oriental tales in the *Rambler* (Nos. 38, 65, 120, 190 and 204-205). It is a moral tale stressing the brevity of human life, so it need not be wasted. Through the fictitious character, Obidah the son of Abensita, in the plains of Indostan, Johnson warns young people not to waste their time. A favoured mid-eighteenth-century topic of discourse is often the question of laziness as a human trait, and Johnson too often dwells on it in his periodical essays. In fact, he frequently reflected on his own alleged inactivity and throughout his life remained critical of procrastination. In 1758 Johnson named a set of one hundred and three periodical essays he wrote in the course of two years *The Idler* (1758-1760) and in No 1 (Saturday, 15 April 1758) he explained how he chose his pen name. 'Every man is', he said, 'or hopes to be, an Idler.' And then after he painted the characteristics of an Idler 'who habituates himself to be satisfied with what he can most easily obtain, not only escapes labours which are often fruitless, but sometimes succeeds better than those who despise all that is within their reach, and think everything more valuable as it is harder to be acquired', he is ready to tease out the slightest nuances of the notion.

To convince the reader that life must not be wasted, in *Rambler* 65 Johnson resorts to the ability of the mind to record experiences at the moment of observation, which he then frames within literary conventions such as plot, setting, narrative structure, characters, mood, theme and moral; and literary techniques such as various types of imagery. Thus, we need to consider how he employs them in a premeditated way in order to transform this simple story into an artful narrative with moral meaning.

First, Johnson deploys literary elements on the basis of their inherent existence. The plot is quite simple – a day in the life of Obidah and his unexpected meeting with the hermit. The setting is artistically contrived and refers to time and place while the narrative structure follows logical order from morning to mid-day to sunset, all in view of a moral theme in mind: 'Human life is a journey that could be compressed to a day and must not be wasted'. As to favoured literary techniques, Johnson uses carefully chosen words and phrases to help him achieve first clarity of expression and secondly and not less important, visual presence of the text with a didactic aim. A supporter of the Baconian ethos of accessibility of literary style reaching a wider audience, Johnson saw his role of a writer as populariser of knowledge in the most accessible form. This is a stand he clearly articulated in his approval of the decision of Joseph Addison (1672-1719) to present 'knowledge in the most alluring form, not lofty and austere, but accessible and familiar', as it 'might prepare the mind for more attainments' (Life of Addison). Similarly, the familiar imagery in Johnson's allegory ties up to the chosen figurative language to create visual representations of actions, objects and ideas that stimulate the physical senses.

Indeed, the visual imagery appeals to the various senses: the colourful description of scenery pertains to the sense of sight; that is further enriched by auditory imagery, that of singing birds and a variety of other noises in nature; to those is added olfactory imagery linked with earthy odours that engage the sense of smell while the gustatory imagery, that of juicy fruits arouses the sense of taste. Johnson also includes tactile imagery linked to physical textures or the sense of touch; for example, as the boy 'plucked the flowers that covered the banks on either side, or the fruits that hung upon the branches'. Further still, the story abounds with kinaesthetic imagery pertaining to movements – the reader follows the young man's constant bodily motion from walking at varied pace, meandering along the craggy paths, turning aside, prostrating himself on the ground in despair to wandering through the wild and advancing towards the light. Last but not least, Johnson employs organic or subjective imagery, linked to the personal experiences of the protagonist that includes his emotions and his awoken senses of hunger, thirst, fatigue and pain. Thus, in using all types of imagery that employ the senses, by evoking movement, space, temperature and personal sense of fatigue, as a true fiction writer, Johnson succeeds in engaging also the readers' senses and lets them envision and relive the story of Obidah.

It needs to be noted that Johnson uses here experimental psychology that is influenced by the philosophy of John Locke (1632-1704), who in *Essay Concerning Human Understanding* offered an analysis of the human mind and the process of its acquisition of knowledge. According to Locke, through experience of the world the mind is able to examine, compare and combine ideas in different ways through sensation. Some of the ideas resemble their causes such as texture, number, size, shape, motion and they are of primary quality; while others such as colour, sound, taste and odour do not, and these are of secondary quality and they depend very much on the primary quality. There is no doubt, that in this allegory, Johnson teases the ability of the mind to conjure up images on the basis of the experience of the senses; in the opinion of Locke, the mind is *tabula rasa*, a blank tablet, and inward ideas are the result of outward sensations; but simple ideas can be converted into more complex ones. In *The Dictionary*, Johnson shows idea n.s as to be derived from French '[idée, French; "d‹a.]', defines it as 'Mental imagination' and uses a quotation from Locke to illustrate it: 'Whatsoever the mind perceives in itself, or is the immediate object of perception, thought, or understanding'. The influence of Locke's philosophical ideas on education, religious toleration and systems of government on eighteenth-century thought is acknowledged by critics. It is also recognised that Locke was a close friend of Newton whose revolutionary discoveries in science were determinant factors in Locke's philosophy. It is further known that Johnson possessed a copy of Locke's *Works* and used illustrations from a variety of sources in *The Dictionary*. In his study of the philosophical words in *The Dictionary* and *The Rambler*, W Wimsatt examined Johnson's frequent usage of Bacon and Locke amongst others and counted 3,200 quotations from Locke (*Philosophic Words*, 1968). Many academic articles have been written highlighting Johnson's respect for Locke's philosophy on human understanding. What has not been discussed though is the imaginative way in which Johnson subsumes Locke's ideas in his periodical essays for the purpose of teaching and that endorses his artistic creativity.

Notably, experimental philosophy demanded new methodology and with it a new set of conventions. In using new allusions and metaphorical expressions, the role of the writer was to transform empirical reality on the poetic canvas and replace the gods and goddesses, the shepherds and shepherdesses, the courtly lovers and ladies of poetic tradition. Thus, the disposition of Johnson's critical mind could not be gratified with 'the remote allusions and obscure opinions' in Milton *Lycidas*. Written in the form of the pastoral, the idyllic imagery of 'smiling plenty', 'rural gaiety' and 'fanciful narratives of superstitious ignorance' was simply no longer acceptable. Eager to observe and understand the laws of nature, the poetic imagination is no longer satisfied with 'the visionary schemes' of pastoral idyll. For Johnson, the allusions from old mythology have lost their credibility, and the idyllic imagery of 'smiling plenty', 'rural gaiety' and 'fanciful narratives of superstitious ignorance have 'no nature', thus, 'no truth'. In *Rasselas*, Nekayah's personal encounter with the outside world has led her to a revision of her general outlook, and she promises to allow herself no more 'to play the shepherdess' in her dreams or to sooth her thoughts with the quiet innocence of 'a lamb entangled in the thicket'. It is not surprising then that Johnson finds Shakespeare's imagery not to be just a mere accumulation of data, but a poetic abstraction of reality. For this, the bard's works may appeal to observation and experience, but their merit lies in the tension between experienced reality and the pleasures of the imagination.

Significantly, the literary topography in *Rambler* 65 also reveals Johnson's art of mapping that offers a spatial model with universal connotation standing apart from any distinct cultural tradition; and this gives a universal appeal to the story. The allegory's imagery of the physical world, for example, is loaded with significant metaphorical meanings as each of the depicted topographical scenes responds not only to the time of day but also corresponds to the different stages in life, from the innocence of the young and the vigour of the middle age to the decrepit old one. The topographical perspective perceives literary space as imaginary geography that allows for space to be deduced as product of human perception, leading to a conclusion with moral values. Johnson's pallet of a true artist allows him to paint varied sceneries that abound in colour and light.

Finally, with the introduction of the hermit near the end of the narrative, Johnson subjects the plot to a twist which heightens the suspense in the reader and gives the story an expected direction. At the point of utter distress and despair, ready to lie down in resignation, Obidiah suddenly sees a light. In *The Dictionary*, 'light n.s.' refers equally to 'a quality of the medium of sight' as to 'illumination of mind; knowledge; instruction'. Thus, the physical presence of light is also charged with a metaphorical meaning, that of knowledge revealed by Obidiah's communication with the hermit. Here Johnson touches upon mid-eighteenth-century sensibilities when the figure of the hermit, a constant figure in English literature since Anglo-Saxon times, experienced a revival in eighteenth-century literature with poems by Thomas Parnell (1679-1718), Oliver Goldsmith (1728-1774), and William Shenstone (1714-1763). A person 'who retires from society to contemplation and devotion' (*The Dictionary*), the hermit became popular in art, literature and garden landscape with fashionable follies with hermitages. However, Johnson did not have time for such veneration and expressed his view on various occasions. In humorous poetic sketch, he said: 'Hermit hoar, in solemn cell/ Wearing out life's evening gray. Strike thy bosom, sage, and tell "What is bliss, and which the way?" Thus I spoke, and speaking sighed, Scarce suppressed the starting tear: When the hoary sage replied, "Come, my lad, and drink some beer" (*Life*)'. Johnson firmly believed that humans were formed for society and need to be in useful service to it. In *Sermon XIII*, for example, he compared 'piety' practised in solitude with a 'flower that blooms in the desert', which gives 'its fragrance to the winds of Heaven' but 'bestows no assistance to earthly beings'. Whether retirement is a desertion of duty, or whether it could be justified as a means for reviewing one's life is a question that Johnson leaves open. Generally he found no excuse for anyone who retreated into a monastic institution expect those 'whose employment is consistent with abstraction, and who, tho' solitary, will not be idle'. In his opinion, those who could justify to retire from public life are either the ones 'whom infirmity makes useless to the commonwealth' or those who have already 'paid their proportion to society, and who, having lived for others', may be honourably dismissed to live for themselves' (*Idler* 38).

Similarly, in this allegory, Johnson portrays the hermit as a man of wisdom who in a gesture of spiritual benevolence is ready to communicate his advice to the young man in order to help him find his way. Hence after a brief dialogue follows his soliloquy that contains the moral of the story deduced afresh and charged with high spiritual overtones.

> 'Go now, my son, to thy repose, commit thyself to the care of omnipotence,
> and when the morning calls again to toil, begin anew thy journey and thy life'

There is much warmth in the tenor of the old man whose powerful words have moral connotation; reformative in nature, they aim to persuade the young man to value his time and leave idleness behind in the course of life, guided by the unbounded power of divine wisdom. A solitary figure, dedicated to contemplation and devotion the hermit is awe inspiring. With no particular religion, he strikes with his deeply felt humanity that has universal resonance; yet his godlike figure adds a spiritual dimension to the young man's journey of self-discovery.

No doubt, the allegory is a testimony of Johnson's creative artistic ability to deliver his credo as a writer in pursuit of the advancement of knowledge in accessible and pleasurable way.

Pleasures of the Imagination   77   Samuel Johnson Illustrated

THE RAMBLER
No 65. Tuesday, 30 October 1750

— — *Garrit aniles*
Ex re fabellas. — —

HORACE, Satires, II.6.77.

The cheerful sage, when solemn dictates fail,
   Conceals the moral counsel in a tale.

Prelude to Rambler No. 65,
by Svetlan Stefanov

Obidah, the son of Abensina, left the caravansera early in the morning, and pursued his journey through the plains of Indostan. He was fresh and vigorous with rest; he was animated with hope; he was incited by desire; he walked swiftly forward over the valleys, and saw the hills gradually rising before him. As he passed along, his ears were delighted with the morning song of the bird of paradise, he was fanned by the last flutters of the sinking breeze, and sprinkled with dew by groves of spices; he sometimes contemplated the towering height of the oak, monarch of the hills; and sometimes caught the gentle fragrance of the primrose, eldest daughter of the spring; all his senses were gratified, and all care was banished from his heart.

The Morning

Thus he went on till the sun approached his meridian, and the increasing heat preyed upon his strength; he then looked round about him for some more commodious path. He saw, on his right hand, a grove that seemed to wave its shades as a sign of invitation; he entered it, and found the coolness and verdure irresistibly pleasant. He did not, however, forget whither he was travelling, but found a narrow way bordered with flowers, which appeared to have the same direction with the main road, and was pleased that, by this happy experiment, he had found means to unite pleasure with business, and to gain the rewards of diligence without suffering its fatigues.

Obidah on the Hills

He, therefore, still continued to walk for a time, without the least remission of his ardour, except that he was sometimes tempted to stop by the music of the birds whom the heat had assembled in the shade; and sometimes amused himself with plucking the flowers that covered the banks on either side, or the fruits that hung upon the branches. At last the green path began to decline from its first tendency, and to wind among hills and thickets, cooled with fountains and murmuring with waterfalls. Here Obidah paused for a time, and began to consider whether it were longer safe to forsake the known and common track; but remembering that the heat was now in its greatest violence, and that the plain was dusty and uneven, he resolved to pursue the new path, which he supposed only to make a few meanders, in compliance with the varieties of the ground, and to end at last in the common road.

The Sunset

Having thus calmed his solicitude, he renewed his pace, though he suspected that he was not gaining ground. This uneasiness of his mind inclined him to lay hold on every new object, and give way to every sensation that might sooth or divert him. He listened to every echo, he mounted every hill for a fresh prospect, he turned aside to every cascade, and pleased himself with tracing the course of a gentle river that rolled among the trees, and watered a large region with innumerable circumvolutions. In these amusements the hours passed away uncounted, his deviations had perplexed his memory, and he knew not towards what point to travel. He stood pensive and confused, afraid to go forward lest he should go wrong, yet conscious that the time of loitering was now past.

The power of Nature

While he was thus tortured with uncertainty, the sky was overspread with clouds, the day vanished from before him, and a sudden tempest gathered round his head. He was now roused by his danger to a quick and painful remembrance of his folly; he now saw how happiness is lost when ease is consulted; he lamented the unmanly impatience that prompted him to seek shelter in the grove, and despised the petty curiosity that led him on from trifle to trifle. While he was thus reflecting, the air grew blacker, and a clap of thunder broke his meditation.

He now resolved to do what remained yet in his power, to tread back the ground which he had passed, and try to find some issue where the wood might open into the plain. He prostrated himself on the ground, and commended his life to the Lord of nature. He rose with confidence and tranquillity, and pressed on with his sabre in his hand, for the beasts of the desert were in motion, and on every hand were heard the mingled howls of rage and fear, and ravage and expiration; all the horrors of darkness and solitude surrounded him; the winds roared in the woods, and the torrents tumbled from the hills,

The air grew blacker

— —χειμαρροι ποταμοι κατ' ορεσφι ρεοντες
Ες μισγαγκειαν συμβαλλετον οβριμον ύδωρ,
Τονδε τε τηλοσε δουπον εν ουρεσιν εκλυε ποιμην.
                    ILIAD, iv.452-53,55

Work'd into sudden rage by wintry show'rs,
Down the steep hill the roaring torrent pours;
The mountain shepherd hears the distant noise.

In the cradle of the night

Thus forlorn and distressed, he wandered through the wild, without knowing whither he was going, or whether he was every moment drawing nearer to safety or to destruction. At length not fear but labour began to overcome him; his breath grew short, and his knees trembled, he was on the point of lying down in resignation to his fate, when he beheld through the brambles the glimmer of a taper.

He advanced towards the light, and finding that it proceeded from the cottage of a hermit, he called humbly at the door, and obtained admission.

The old man set before him such provisions as he had collected for himself, on which Obidah fed with eagerness and gratitude.

When the repast was over, "Tell me," said the hermit, "by what chance thou hast been brought hither; I have been now twenty years an inhabitant of the wilderness, in which I never saw a man before." Obidah then related the occurrences of his journey, without any concealment or palliation.

The morning is still to come

"Son," said the hermit, "let the errors and follies, the dangers and escape of this day, sink deep into thy heart. Remember, my son, that human life is the journey of a day. We rise in the morning of youth, full of vigour and full of expectation; we set forward with spirit and hope, with gaiety and with diligence, and travel on a while in the straight road of piety towards the mansions of rest. In a short time we remit our fervour, and endeavour to find some mitigation of our duty, and some more easy means of obtaining the same end.

We then relax our vigour, and resolve no longer to be terrified with crimes at a distance, but rely upon our own constancy, and venture to approach what we resolve never to touch. We thus enter the bowers of ease, and repose in the shades of security.

Here the heart softens and vigilance subsides; we are then willing to inquire whether another advance cannot be made, and whether we may not, at least, turn our eyes upon the gardens of pleasure. We approach them with scruple and hesitation; we enter them, but enter timorous and trembling, and always hope to pass through them without losing the road of virtue, which we, for a while, keep in our sight, and to which we propose to return.

But temptation succeeds temptation, and one compliance prepares us for another; we in time lose the happiness of innocence, and solace our disquiet with sensual gratifications. By degrees we let fall the remembrance of our original intention, and quit the only adequate object of rational desire.

We entangle ourselves in business, immerge ourselves in luxury, and rove through the labyrinths of inconstancy, till the darkness of old age begins to invade us, and disease and anxiety obstruct our way. We then look back upon our lives with horrour, with sorrow, with repentance; and wish, but too often vainly wish, that we had not forsaken the ways of virtue.

Happy are they, my son, who shall learn from thy example not to despair, but shall remember, that though the day is past, and their strength is wasted, there yet remains one effort to be made; that reformation is never hopeless, nor sincere endeavours ever unassisted; that the wanderer may at length return after all his errors, and that he who implores strength and courage from above, shall find danger and difficulty give way before him.

Go now, my son, to thy repose, commit thyself to the care of Omnipotence, and when the morning calls again to toil, begin anew thy journey and thy life."

In the steps of the Old Man

THE RAMBLER
No. 67. Tuesday, 6 November 1750

Frontispiece, The Gentleman's Magazine, Vol. XXV (1755)

THE RAMBLER
No. 67. Tuesday, 6 November 1750

The Garden of Hope - A Dream.

Brief Analytical Notes

Rambler 67 is an allegorical essay in which Johnson plays with the idea of a dream as a literary device. In *The Dictionary* Johnson defines 'dream' in the following way: 'DREAM.n.s.[droom, Dutch. This word is derived by Meric Casaubon, with more ingenuity than truth, from *dqŠla sot b'ot*, the comedy of life; dreams being, as plays are, a representation of something which does not really happen. This conceit Junius has enlarged by quoting an epigram.' In other words, imaginary activities take place while the mind is in a state of sleep, 'a phantasm of sleep' or 'an idle fancy'. But while in a real dream situation ideas may come in no particular order, in this fictitious piece they take shape in a pre-determined and carefully organised structure.

It should be also remembered that to the mid-eighteenth-century mind the notion of a dream or the act of dreaming had much deeper connotation that engaged the philosophical question of 'does the soul think?' Isaac Newton's theories of physics (The Three Universal Laws of Motion, the *Principia*, 1687) had led to the pressing dilemma of the materiality or immateriality of the soul. That Johnson himself was interested in the issue is confirmed, for example, by his discussion on it in *Rasselas,* Ch xlviii, 'Imlac discourses on the Nature of the Soul' (1759). 'Of immateriality', said Imlac [in his role of an Eastern poet and philosopher], 'our ideas are negative, and therefore obscure. Immateriality seems to imply a natural power of perpetual duration as a consequence of exemption from all causes of decay'. Following his contemplation on the nature of the soul, Imlac decidedly resolved that 'an ideal form is no less real than material bulk' and gave an example with the concept of a pyramid which when created in the mind had no extension, yet the image of it was no less real than the physical object of it.

Further, the physical or metaphysical nature of the soul was not only a pertinent post-Newtonian philosophical question that was touching upon the issue of materialism and that of deism (a denial of all revealed religion); it was also closely linked with the idea of creative thought. Newton had also shown that in the process of discovery, reason could prove insufficient. When he came to formulate his universal laws of nature, to the value of experimental, for the benefit of the philosophical argument, the intuitive impulse of 'anticipation' became an integral part of his mental vision, that of 'seeing that' in the 'mind's eye'. In *Adventurer* 131 Johnson expressed his high respect for the peculiar bend of Newton's intellectual abilities and justly remarked that 'Newton's superiority to the rest of mankind' stemmed from his ability to 'separate knowledge from those weaknesses by which knowledge is generally disgraced'; and his incomparability was, in Johnson's words, 'not because he [Newton] deviated from the beaten track', but because he bravely 'stood alone, merely because he had left the rest of mankind behind him'.

Johnson describes this type of creativity as 'a sensibility of perfection which touched fibres of the mental texture'; an act of the imagination which is performed 'before reason can descend from her throne, to pass her sentence' (*Idler* 78). Indeed, the difference 'between Idea and Reality' often occupied Johnson's attention. For instance, in a letter to his young friend Bennet Langton he wrote: 'I know not anything more pleasant or more instructive than to compare experience with expectation' (*Life*, 27 June 1758). In some of his periodical essays Johnson projects his mind into an imaginary state of a dreaming person, as is the case with *Rambler* 67 where by putting himself in the position of a first person narrator he lets the linguistic and discursive give rise to the pictorial and figural. And as word and image overlap, it becomes a pleasure journey and the reader is drawn into its imaginative reconstruction.

Johnson creates a vivid composition in which he resorts to an aerial perspective to allow for a 'more extensive view of the whole place', and the depiction acquires cinematographic effect. The fast moving scenes heighten the reader's suspense, while the presence of the two monsters gives the story somewhat gothic resonance. But beneath these simple on the surface entertaining conventions, as a writer with a social agenda, Johnson weaves his reflections on the meaning of 'hope'. In *The Dictionary* the definition of the word is as follows: HOPE.n.s. [hopa, Saxon; hope, Dutch] as 'Expectation of some good; an expectation indulged with pleasure'. The illustrative quotation is by John Locke (1634-1704), from *The Two Treatises of Government* (1690) which has been long hailed a seminal work in the history of political liberalism. It reads: 'Hope is that pleasure in the mind which every one finds in himself, upon the thought of a profitable future enjoyment of a thing, which is apt to delight him', underlining the universal nature of this abstract idea that is so deeply engrained in the human psyche. Locke conveyed a clear social message in his discourse in that the state's prerogative was the welfare of people on the path to good fortune, success and prosperity, and poverty was insupportable without provision of the basic necessaries of life.

That Johnson's concern for the poor was never far from his mind is evident from a variety of his writings on poverty and his expressed concern for those who lived at the margins of society – a strand that has yet to be fully appreciated. Boswell, for example, spoke of Johnson's compassion for the bleak prospects of those who, impoverished and faced with dire economic circumstance, were reduced to begging. 'You meet a man begging, you charge him with idleness: he says, 'I am willing to labour. Will you give me work?' – 'I cannot.' – 'Why, then you have no right to charge me with idleness.' Through his writings Johnson gave voice to those impoverished members of society: a hungry family at times of bad harvest, a debtor languishing in prison or a young girl driven to prostitution – all forced by societal conditions into a marginal existence. He often argued that 'the miseries of poverty, of sickness, of captivity' would be 'insupportable' without hope and that 'hope is necessary in every condition'. In *Rambler* 67, too, the scenes that unfold on the vast poetic canvas touch upon the inherent human trait of incessant want and Johnson's reflections on the fallacious nature of hope acquire a much deeper social meaning.

Against the backdrop of a crowd of all ages, sexes and race, hurriedly moving in their pursuit of happiness, *Rambler 67* has a universal appeal, but it can be also read as a thought provoking critique of the ills of eighteenth-century society. Through the ugly monster Want Johnson captures the disquiet of society which was undergoing rapid social changes in structure and behaviour as the process of industrialization was gathering pace. New sources of wealth resulted in the growth of a middle class and a visible presence of the industrious poor who were denied opportunities to better lives. In *The Dictionary*, WANT.n.s. relates to '1. Need.' and is supported with a quotation by Locke, 'Parents should distinguish between the wants of fancy, and those of nature' that highlights the polar meaning of the word: that of fancy led by greed and idleness and that of the natural right of man as specified in sense 3, 'The state of not having' and sense 4: 'Poverty; penury; indigence. Nothing is so hard for those who abound in riches, as to conceive how others can be in want'. Johnson often exposed the desire of selfish accumulation of wealth, as he put it in *Sermon* 4, those who were 'blessed with abundance, and reveling in delight, yet overborne by ungovernable desires of encreasing acquisitions... to pile heaps on heaps, and add one superfluity to another'.

As a moral writer, Johnson is keen to help the reader grasp some critical attributes of hope and he uses personifications. The garden of Hope is flanked by two guarded gates, one by Reason, the other by Fancy. He directs his criticism to those travelers who, attracted by the gentle and easy manners of Fancy were unwilling to put any contrastive efforts and readily entered 'the Vale of Idleness'. Reason, on the other hand, is personified as a surly deity, unwilling to let anyone easily through her gate, and was subjecting all to the Straight of Difficulty, 'a craggy, slippery, and winding path'. The journey is marred by 'a thousand intricacies' so that those who succeeded in obtaining the 'gift of Hope' regretted their efforts and retired in the 'bowers of Content' in perpetual inactivity. The 'inaccessible steep' topographic imagery of the path to Reason is juxtaposed with the smooth and gentle passage to Fancy who offered easy access to her dominion and her followers were seen to be 'making themselves wings, which others were 'contriving to actuate by the perpetual motion' alluding to the eighteenth-century yearning for flying and ongoing related experimentations.

As a true master of language, Johnson is able to select and use words for their kindred senses. Executed via the medium of a dream, the allegory strikes with its structural integrity of a whole where the soul makes itself known through images, colours, shapes, textures and ideas. Moving from one medium to another, from that of sight to that of hearing, smell, taste and touch Johnson proves a true painter of nature. To the abundance of colour is added that of light, while depth and motion make the writing essentially visual, pictorial and cinematographic.

The allegory ends with the sudden awakening of the author where the 'universal shriek of affright' expresses a climax of everyman's emotional experience. In *The Dictionary* 'affright n.s.' signifies 'terror; fear'. The remark that the word is 'chiefly poetical' confirms that Johnson chose to use it in order to enhance the utmost state of inner psychological upheaval of the mind. Here it can be taken as an anticipation of something frightful; in this case the sight of Want and Age for Johnson, a writer with acute social morality, are metaphors that stand for insatiable human greed as well as deplorable miseries exacerbated by physical and mental frailties of age.

The words conjure up an unbearable image in the mind's consciousness; thus, the awakening can be taken as an encoded call for action on Johnson's part as a writer with a social agenda.

THE RAMBLER
No. 67. Tuesday, 6 November 1750

Αι δ' ελπιδες βοσκουσι φυγαδας, ὡς λογος
Καλοις βλεπουσι γ' ομμασιν, μελλουσι δε.

EURIPIDES, Phoenissae, II. 396-97.

Exiles, the proverb says, subsist on hope,
Delusive hope still points to distant good,
To good that mocks approach.

Prelude to Rambler No. 67, by Svetlan Stefanov

There is no temper so generally indulged as hope: other passions operate by starts on particular occasions, or in certain parts of life; but hope begins with the first power of comparing our actual with our possible state, and attends us through every stage and period, always urging us forward to new acquisitions, and holding out some distant blessing to our view, promising us either relief from pain, or increase of happiness.

Hope

Hope is necessary in every condition. The miseries of poverty, of sickness, of captivity, would, without this comfort, be insupportable; nor does it appear that the happiest lot of terrestrial existence can set us above the want of this general blessing; or that life, when the gifts of nature and of fortune are accumulated upon it, would not still be wretched, were it not elevated and delighted by the expectation of some new possession, of some enjoyment yet behind, by which the wish shall be at last satisfied, and the heart filled up to its utmost extent.

Hope, is indeed, very fallacious, and promises what it seldom gives; but its promises are more valuable than the gifts of fortune, and it seldom frustrates us without assuring us of recompensing the delay by a greater bounty.

I was musing on this strange inclination which every man feels to deceive himself, and considering the advantages and dangers proceeding from this gay prospect of futurity, when, falling asleep, on a sudden I found myself placed in a garden, of which my sight could descry no limits. Every scene about me was gay and gladsome, light with sunshine, and fragrant with perfumes; the ground was painted with all the variety of spring, and all the choir of nature was singing in the groves. When I had recovered from the first raptures, with which the confusion of pleasure had for a time entranced me, I began to take a particular and deliberate view of this delightful region.

I then perceived that I had yet higher gratifications to expect, and that, at a small distance from me, there were brighter flowers, clearer fountains, and more lofty groves, where the birds, which I yet heard but faintly, were exerting all the power of melody. The trees about me were beautiful with verdure, and fragrant with blossoms; but I was tempted to leave them by the sight of ripe fruits, which seemed to hang only to be plucked. I therefore walked hastily forwards, but found, as I proceeded, that the colours of the field faded at my approach, the fruit fell before I reached it, the birds flew still singing before me, and though I pressed onward with great celerity, I was still in sight of pleasures of which I could not yet gain the possession, and which seemed to mock my diligence, and to retire as I advanced.

The Dream

Though I was confounded with so many alternations of joy and grief, I yet persisted to go forward, in hopes that these fugitive delights would in time be overtaken. At length I saw an innumerable multitude of every age and sex, who seemed all to partake of some general felicity; for every cheek was flushed with confidence, and every eye sparkled with eagerness: yet each appeared to have some particular and secret pleasure, and very few were willing to communicate their intentions, or extend their concern beyond themselves. Most of them seemed, by the rapidity of their motion, too busy to gratify the curiosity of a stranger, and therefore I was content for a while to gaze upon them, without interrupting them with troublesome inquiries. At last I observed one man worn with time, and unable to struggle in the crowd; and, therefore, supposing him more at leisure, I began to accost him: but he turned from me with anger, and told me he must not be disturbed, for the great hour of projection was now come when Mercury should lose his wings, and slavery should no longer dig the mine for gold.

The chains of Slavery

I left him, and attempted another, whose softness of mien, and easy movement, gave me reason to hope for a more agreeable reception; but he told me, with a low bow, that nothing would make him more happy than an opportunity of serving me, which he could not now want, for a place which he had been twenty years soliciting would be soon vacant. From him I had recourse to the next, who was departing in haste to take possession of the estate of an uncle, who by the course of nature could not live long. He that followed was preparing to dive for treasure in a new-invented bell; and another was on the point of discovering the longitude.

Science

Being thus rejected wheresoever I applied myself for information, I began to imagine it best to desist from inquiry, and try what my own observation would discover: but seeing a young man, gay and thoughtless, I resolved upon one more experiment, and was informed that I was in the garden of Hope, and daughter of Desire, and that all those whom I saw thus tumultuously bustling round me were incited by the promises of Hope, and hastening to seize the gifts which she held in her hand.

I turned my sight upward, and saw a goddess in the bloom of youth sitting on a throne: around her lay all the gifts of fortune, and all the blessings of life were spread abroad to view; she had a perpetual gaiety of aspect, and every one imagined that her smile, which was impartial and general, was directed to himself, and triumphed in his own superiority to others, who had conceived the same confidence from the same mistake.

I then mounted an eminence, from which I had a more extensive view of the whole place, and could with less perplexity consider the different conduct of the crowds that filled it. From this station I observed, that the entrance into the garden of Hope was by two gates, one of which was kept by Reason, and the other by Fancy. Reason was surly and scrupulous, and seldom turned the key without many interrogatories, and long hesitation; but Fancy was a kind and gentle portress, she held her gate wide open, and welcomed all equally to the district under her superintendency; so that the passage was crowded by all those who either feared the examination of Reason, or had been rejected by her.

From the gate of Reason there was a way to the throne of Hope, by a craggy, slippery and winding path, called the Streight of Difficulty, which those who entered with the permission of the guard endeavoured to climb.

But though they surveyed the way very carefully before they began to rise, and marked out the several stages of their progress, they commonly found unexpected obstacles, and were obliged frequently to stop on the sudden, where they imagined the way plain and even.

A thousand intricacies embarrassed them, a thousand slips threw them back, and a thousand pitfalls impeded their advance.

So formidable were the dangers, and so frequent the miscarriages, that many returned from the first attempt, and many fainted in the midst of the way, and only a very small number were led up to the summit of Hope, by the hand of Fortitude. Of these few the greater part, when they had obtained the gift which Hope had promised them, regretted the labour which it cost, and felt in their success the regret of disappointment; the rest retired with their prize, and were led by Wisdom to the bowers of Content.

Turning then towards the gate of Fancy, I could find no way to the seat of Hope; but though she sat full in view, and held out her gifts with an air of invitation, which filled every heart with rapture, the mountain was, on that side, inaccessibly steep, but so channelled and shaded, that none perceived the impossibility of ascending it, but each imagined himself to have discovered a way to which the rest were strangers.

Many expedients were indeed tried by this industrious tribe, of whom some were making themselves wings, which others were contriving to actuate by the perpetual motion. But with all their labour, and all their artifices, they never rose above the ground, or quickly fell back, nor ever approached the throne of Hope, but continued still to gaze at a distance, and laughed at the slow progress of those whom they saw toiling in the Streight of Difficulty.

Part of the favourites of Fancy, when they had entered the garden, without making, like the rest, an attempt to climb the mountain, turned immediately to the Vale of Idleness, a calm and undisturbed retirement, from whence they could always have Hope in prospect, and to which they pleased themselves with believing that she intended speedily to descend.

These were indeed scorned by all the rest; but they seemed very little affected by contempt, advice, or reproof, but were resolved to expect at ease the favour of the goddess.

At the gates of Fancy and Reason

Among this gay race I was wandering, and found them ready to answer all my questions, and willing to communicate their mirth; but turning round, I saw two dreadful monsters entering the vale, one of whom I knew to be Age, and the other Want.

The two Beasts

Sport and revelling were now at an end, and an universal shriek of affright and distress burst out and awaked me.

The Awakening from a Nightmare (Il.S. Stefanov)

THE RAMBLER
No. 102. Saturday, 9 March 1751

Frontispiece, The Gentleman's Magazine, Vol. XXV (1755)

THE RAMBLER
No. 102. Saturday, 9 March 1751

The meaning of life - A dream.

Brief Analytical Notes

This allegory takes the form of a dream in which Johnson uses ocean topography to map out the stages of human life, from infancy to the folly of youth to manhood and the state of the ocean's cyclic rise and fall serves as an indicator of the passage of time.

To appeal to the general reader, Johnson's choice of nautical imagery is not coincidental. During the eighteenth century Britain saw a huge expansion in sea trade and as each year ships with goods sailed between Asia and Europe, there were often shipwrecks that led to a loss of human lives and valuable cargoes. There were stories in the public domain about the ten-month voyage to Calcutta, Bombay or Madras and then on to Canton for tea and porcelain. Just as treacherous were the tides and winds of the English Channel which brought about shocking and widely reported news of shipwrecks in the daily press. The dangers of sea travel came closer to home when Johnson's younger brother Nathaniel (1712-1737) who had planned to emigrate to Georgia at the age of twenty four, only reached as far as Frome in Somerset and returned home. Years later, Johnson's servant Frank Barber would run away to sea (1758) and Johnson would plead to the Admiralty for his release, deploring the intolerable living and working conditions on board by saying that 'being in a ship, is like being in a jail, with the chance of being drowned' (*Life*). As to literature, Daniel Defoe's *Robinson Crusoe* (1719) had run through a few editions in the eighteenth century. Johnson was familiar with the novel and thought that it was 'enough to establish his [Defoe's] reputation' (ibid).

Further still, the primordial ocean symbolises beginning of life on our planet. 'Primordial' constitutes an origin, and is defined as 'existing from the beginning' in *The Dictionary*. Johnson's allusions to 'the tumult of labour, the shouts of alacrity, the shrieks of alarm', together with 'the whistle of the winds and the dash of waters' in this allegory, are suggestive of birth, of primeval existence. The primordial ocean also relates to the subconscious mind, that great intuitive power within, a source of creativity, a state of human 'astonishment' that is carried on the wings of poetic imagination in a sudden bout of vigorous intellectual and artistic experience. Moreover, the primordial ocean is a universal symbol shared by the human collective unconscious and that gives the allegory a universal dimension.

Distinct topographic oceanic characteristics are imaginatively and vividly reconstructed into literary devices. 'The Straights of Infancy', strewn with fragile vessels and reckless multitudes, come to characterise the folly and inexperience of early age; whereas the quickly rushing waves in the Gulph of Intemperance, with dangerous whirlpools and the Rocks of Pleasure conjure up images of instability and disturbance and allude to a phase of rapid change in the middle years of human life. Significantly, the final frontier of the voyage of life regardless of its length remains death which from the start of the allegory is integral to Johnson's notion of life and the related incidents. The moral tone used by him to describe each one, draws poetic power and legitimacy from a predetermined, inevitable end and exposes the stark contradictions in human nature. Propelled by curiosity and desire for invention, the human psyche strives for knowledge; but when that becomes entangled with the innate human trait of incessant want, the latter is hard to control.

Aesthetically, the created nautical scene of violent storm and rough seas touches upon the sublime, a kind of pleasurable terror – an idea that Edmund Burke (1729-1797) would discuss a few years later in *A Philosophical Enquiry into the Origin of Our Ideas of the Sublime and Beautiful* (1757). Johnson thought highly of the enquiry of Burke who became a member of Johnson's Literary Club (founded 1764) and a lifelong friend. Burke divided his discourse into seven aspects, all of which he argued were discernible in the natural world, thus natural phenomena: Darkness – which constrains the sense of sight (primary among the five senses); Obscurity – which confuses judgement; Privation (or deprivation) – since pain is more powerful than pleasure; Vastness – which is beyond comprehension; Magnificence – in the face of which we are in awe; Loudness – which overwhelms us; Suddenness – which shocks our sensibilities to the point of disablement. It can be said that in his allegory Johnson engages the Burkean aesthetic aspects to create a contemplation that transports the spectator beyond the natural and elevates the mind.

The composition of *Rambler* 102 strikes with its powerful conception that is further enhanced by the artistic stimulus of powerful and inspired emotion and added choice of words and distinct perspicuity of style; they all help create the grandeur of imagery. Johnson's nautical scapes are reminiscent of the type of sublimity found in the awe-inspiring painting *The Shipwreck* (1805) by JMW Turner (1775-1851). The sense of the massive scale of the vast ocean is contrasted by the diminutive human figures, accentuating the dramatic effect of human misfortune. The selected viewpoint is away from the shoreline, allowing the viewer to contemplate the storm, to immerse in the raging sea alongside those struggling for survival.

Moreover, the recreated nautical scenes travel across the universal history canon with ease; they are reminiscent of Homer's epic *The Odyssey* and the visionary journey of Dante Alighieri (1265-1321) in the *Divine Comedy*. However, as a true artist, Johnson breeds new life into the idea and creates his own imagery that strives toward permanent values. The abstract ideas of Hope and Reason and their personifications act as an artistic plot device. The Gulph of Intemperance, 'a dreadful whirlpool, interspersed with rocks, of which the pointed crags were concealed under water' was in the misleading dominion of Ease and Pleasure. Reason was attempting to steer her passengers away from the 'Rocks of Pleasure' only to witness their futile struggle. Intense emotions such as horror and terror create a new aesthetic experience that is anchored in the sublimity of the natural world and that is being observed because of its relation to the striving human psyche pushing upwards against overbearing forces beyond the limits of reason. The physical, metaphysical, moral, aesthetic and spiritual become interwoven and our ability to comprehend is overwhelmed.

In brief, the affinity between literature and the visual arts is masterfully exemplified in this allegory in which Johnson rises to the challenge of an artist capable of creating a powerful and inspiring emotion. Moreover, he relates universal perceptions of the relationship between nature and humankind - a pleasurable dread of those embarked on the journey of life drifting aimlessly, unsure of their bearings, unsure indeed if there is anywhere to head. There may be an allusion to a Christian paradigm such as the Deluge, but Johnson skilfully manipulates it and juxtaposes the religious code with that of modern life that is anchored in the eternal present.

The Gulph of Intemperance may have lost the immediacy of its symbolic meaning; but the same thorny issues of excessive drinking and overindulgence in eating are just as pertinent today as they were in the mid-eighteenth century. Modern events also show how a series of political and intellectual cataclysms are leaving multitudes feeling destitute and thus cast adrift. Boats overflowing with immigrants and ships sailing adrift, amid high winds and waves continue to be endangered vessels today which are equally threatened with instant destruction.

In brief, Johnson's *Rambler* 102, anchored in the eternal present, is everyman's personal journey that leads to the transformation of the self. For that the allegory has a worldwide public appeal.

THE RAMBLER
No. 102. Saturday, 9 March 1751

Ipsa quoque assiduo labuntur tempora motu,
Non secus ac flumen. Neque enim consistere flumen,
Nec levis hora potest: sed ut unda impellitur unda,
Urgeturque prior veniente, urgetque priorem,
Tempora sic fugiunt pariter, pariterque sequuntur.

OVID, Metamorphoses. xv. 179-83.

With constant motion as the moments glide.
Behold in running life the rolling tide!
For none can stem by art, or stop by pow'r,
The flowing ocean, or the fleeting hour:
But wave by wave pursued arrives on shore,
And each impell'd behind impels before:
So time on time revolving we descry;
So minutes follow, and so minutes fly.

ELPHINSTON.

Prelude to Rambler No. 102,
by Svetlan Stefanov

"Life," says Seneca, "is a voyage, in the progress of which we are perpetually changing our scenes: we first leave childhood behind us, then youth, then the years of ripened manhood, then the better and more pleasing part of old age." The perusal of this passage having incited in me a train of reflections on the state of man, the incessant fluctuation of his wishes, the gradual change of his disposition to all external objects, and the thoughtlessness with which he floats along the stream of time, I sunk into a slumber amidst my meditations, and on a sudden, found my ears filled with the tumult of labour, the shouts of alacrity, the shrieks of alarm, the whistle of winds, and the dash of waters.

The years of ripened Manhood

My astonishment for a time repressed my curiosity; but soon recovering myself so far as to inquire whither we were going, and what was the cause of such clamour and confusion, I was told that we were launching out into the *ocean of life*; that we had already passed the streights of infancy, in which multitudes had perished, some by the weakness and fragility of their vessels, and more by the folly, perverseness, or negligence, of those who undertook to steer them; and that we were now on the main sea, abandoned to the winds and billows, without any other means of security than the care of the pilot, whom it was always in our power to choose among great numbers that offered their direction and assistance.

I then looked round with anxious eagerness; and first turning my eyes behind me, saw a stream flowing through flowery islands, which every one that sailed along seemed to behold with pleasure; but no sooner touched, than the current, which, though not noisy or turbulent, was yet irresistible, bore him away. Beyond these islands all was darkness, nor could any of the passengers describe the shore at which he first embarked.

The Voyage of Life

Before me, and on each side, was an expanse of waters violently agitated, and covered with so thick a mist, that the most perspicacious eye could see but a little way. It appeared to be full of rocks and whirlpools, for many sunk unexpectedly while they were courting the gale with full sails, and insulting those whom they had left behind. So numerous, indeed, were the dangers, and so thick the darkness, that no caution could confer security. Yet there were many, who, by false intelligence, betrayed their followers into whirlpools, or by violence pushed those whom they found in their way against the rocks.

The current was invariable and insurmountable; but though it was impossible to sail against it, or to return to the place that was once passed, yet it was not so violent as to allow no opportunities for dexterity or courage, since, though none could retreat back from danger, yet they might often avoid it by oblique direction.

It was, however, not very common to steer with much care or prudence; for by some universal infatuation, every man appeared to think himself safe, though he saw his consorts every moment sinking round him; and no sooner had the waves closed over them, than their fate and their misconduct were forgotten; the voyage was pursued with the same jocund confidence; every man congratulated himself upon the soundness of his vessel, and believed himself able to stem the whirlpool in which his friend was swallowed, or glide over the rocks on which he was dashed: nor was it often observed that the sight of a wreck made any man change his course: if he turned aside for a moment, he soon forgot the rudder, and left himself again to the disposal of chance.

In the course of the Voyage of Life

This negligence did not proceed from indifference, or from weariness of their present condition; for not one of those who thus rushed upon destruction, failed, when he was sinking, to call loudly upon his associates for that help which could not now be given him; and many spent their last moments in cautioning others against the folly by which they were intercepted in the midst of their course. Their benevolence was sometimes praised, but their admonitions were unregarded.

The vessels in which we had embarked being confessedly unequal to the turbulence of the stream of life, were visibly impaired in the course of the voyage; so that every passenger was certain, that how long soever he might, by favourable accidents, or by incessant vigilance, be preserved, he must sink at last.

This necessity of perishing might have been expected to sadden the gay, and intimidate the daring, at least to keep the melancholy and timorous in perpetual torments, and hinder them from any enjoyment of the varieties and gratifications which nature offered them as the solace of their labours; yet, in effect, none seemed less to expect destruction than those to whom it was most dreadful; they all had the art of concealing their danger from themselves; and those who knew their inability to bear the sight of the terrors that embarrassed their way, took care never to look forward, but found some amusement for the present moment, and generally entertained themselves by playing with Hope, who was the constant associate of the voyage of life.

Yet all that Hope ventured to promise, even to those whom she favoured most, was not that they should escape, but that they should sink last; and with this promise everyone was satisfied, though he laughed at the rest for seeming to believe it. Hope, indeed, apparently mocked the credulity of her companions; for, in proportion as their vessels grew leaky, she redoubled her assurances of safety; and none were more busy in making provisions for a long voyage, than they whom all but themselves saw likely to perish soon by irreparable decay.

In the midst of the current of life was the Gulph of Intemperance, a dreadful whirlpool, interspersed with rocks, of which the pointed crags were concealed under water, and the tops covered with herbage, on which Ease spread couches of repose, and with shades, where Pleasure warbled the song of invitation. Within sight of these rocks all who sailed on the ocean of life must necessarily pass.

Reason, indeed, was always at hand to steer the passengers through a narrow outlet by which they might escape; but very few could, by her entreaties or remonstrances, be induced to put the rudder into her hand, without stipulating that she should approach so near unto the rocks of Pleasure, that they might solace themselves with a short enjoyment of that delicious region, after which they always determined to pursue their course without any other deviation.

The Gulph of Intemperance

Reason was too often prevailed upon so far by these promises, as to venture her charge within the eddy of the Gulph of Intemperance, where, indeed, the circumvolution was weak, but yet interrupted the course of the vessel, and drew it, by insensible rotations, towards the centre. She then repented her temerity, and with all her force endeavoured to retreat; but the draught of the gulph was generally too strong to be overcome; and the passenger, having danced in circles with a pleasing and giddy velocity, was at last overwhelmed and lost. Those few whom Reason was able to extricate, generally suffered so many shocks upon the points which shot out from the rocks of Pleasure, that they were unable to continue their course with the same strength and facility as before, but floated along timorously and feeble, endangered by every breeze, and shattered by every ruffle of the water, till they sunk, by slow degrees, after long struggles, and innumerable expedients, always repining at their own folly, and warning others against the first approach of the Gulph of Intemperance.

The Rocks of Pleasure

There were artists who professed to repair the breaches and stop the leaks of the vessels which had been shattered on the rocks of

Pleasure. Many appeared to have great confidence in their skill, and some, indeed, were preserved by it from sinking, who had received only a single blow; but I remarked that few vessels lasted long which had been much repaired, nor was it found that the artists themselves continued afloat longer than those who had least of their assistance.

The only advantage which, in the voyage of life, the cautious had above the negligent, was, that they sunk later, and more suddenly; for they passed forward till they had sometimes seen all those in whose company they had issued from the Streights of Infancy, perish in the way, and at last were overset by a cross breeze, without the toil of resistance, or the anguish of expectation. But such as had often fallen against the Rocks of Pleasure, commonly subsided by sensible degrees, contended long with the encroaching waters, and harassed themselves by labours that scarce Hope herself could flatter with success.

The Sudden Awakening

As I was looking upon the various fate of the multitude about me, I was suddenly alarmed with an admonition from some unknown Power, "Gaze not idly upon others when thou thyself art sinking. Whence is this thoughtless tranquillity, when thou and they are equally endangered?"

I looked, and seeing the Gulph of Intemperance before me, started and awaked.

THE VISION OF THEODORE, THE HERMIT OF TENERIFFE, FOUND IN HIS CELL 1748

Frontispiece (after L S Lowry, 1943)
by Stefka Ritchie

Analytical Notes to *The Vision of Theodore, the hermit of Teneriffe, found in his cell* **(1748)**

A. Why Johnson thought *The Vision* was the best piece he ever wrote.

According to Thomas Percy (1729-1811), Johnson 'attributed the palm over all he ever wrote to the little allegorical piece [The Vision]' (Life). This assertion has always been doubted by Johnsonian critics who like to elaborate on possible reasons as to why Bishop Percy (chaplain to George III before being appointed bishop of Dromore, County Down, Ireland; also author of *Reliques of Ancient English Poetry* of 1765) might have made such a remark and some suggest that Johnson might have been joking; or that he might have been referring to his Oriental tales and allegories [the periodical essays of the 1750s] before he wrote Rasselas (1759).

Contrary to prevailing critical opinion, it is argued here that Johnson was right in his high esteem of The Vision. Rather than encompassing the picture of the whole composition and the richness of the text's multiple voices, critics have been fixed on a single point, failing to grasp the unity of the composition and the originality of Johnson's artistic imagination which reflected the sensibilities of his age.

Historical background

First, it should be remembered that The Vision was written during the middle years of Johnson's life which proved fertile for Johnson who had arrived in London in 1737 at the age of twenty eight to make a name for himself as a writer. After the early poem *London* (1738) in imitation of the Third Satire of Juvenal he began contributing to Edward Cave's *The Gentleman's Magazine* and became particularly involved in reporting the Parliamentary debates by composing speeches based on the actual debates ('Debates in the Senate of Lilliput', 1741-1744). Shortly after that Johnson embarked single-handedly on the composition of *The Dictionary* (1746-1755); and during those so called 'middle years' of his life, he wrote The Vision (1748) and *The Preface to The Preceptor* (1749), Robert Dodsley's textbook manual, followed by his finest poem *The Vanity of Human Wishes* (1749), an imitation of Juvenal's Tenth Satire. In the 368 lines of this poem written in closed heroic couplets, he examined the turbulent history of mankind: from the Danube and the Rhine, steeped in blood, to the walls of Moscow, surveying the map of the world with scenes of raging wars extending from 'Persia's tyrant' and 'Bavaria's lord' to the 'daring Greeks' and the 'fierce Croatian'. Johnson's skilful selection of words in the poem produced overtones of meaning that added richness to his interpretation of the universal traits of human nature – those blind illusions and frolics of passions that were driving human beings into a permanent state of war. This was a theme that Johnson had engaged with in the previous year in The Vision of Theodore, the Hermit of Teneriffe found in his cell (The Vision), for short.

Secondly, The Vision was written during the time Johnson was busy with the compilation of The Dictionary (1746-1755). 'The uncertainly of terms, and commixture of ideas, is well known to those who have joined philosophy with grammar', he declared in his Preface to The Dictionary and further elaborated on the complexity of the issue in that 'ideas of the same race, thought exactly alike, are sometimes so little different that no words can express the dissimilitude, though the mind easily perceives it'. These remarks throw light on two major points in Johnson's treatment of words. On one hand, they confirm his recognition of the richness of their signification, as 'kindred senses may be so interwoven'; on the other hand, they affirm his realization of the inability of words to express to the full the thoughts generated in the mind. Indeed, as he strove to provide a 'correct standard of meaning and usage of words', Johnson became particularly aware of the delineated multiple meanings of words under each 'hard' entry, from their 'primitive and natural use' to the more subtle and metaphorical. 'In every word of extensive use', he explained, 'it was requisite to mark the progress of its meaning, and show by what gradations of intermediate sense it has passed from its primitive to its remote and accidental signification'. The statement reaffirms the extent to which Johnson was concerned with finding nuances of meaning for each word, from their most 'primitive' to their most 'accidental'.

There is no doubt that the work on *The Dictionary* would have allowed Johnson to recognize the complexity of word significations which he used to advantage in his allegory The Vision. It would have enabled him to select words with great dexterity for their 'primitive' as well as their 'remote and accidental significations'. I would add to those, for their visual impact too. Thus, 'precipice', 'bowers', 'crags' and 'caverns', 'pines', 'fruits', 'flowers' and 'birds' are amongst the boundless variety of deliberately chosen lexis that conjure up colourful imagery of physical nature, whereas 'chains', pygmies' and 'tyrant' are linked with traits of human nature.

Another important point to be noted is that when Johnson commenced his work on *The Dictionary*, he declared that he was resolved to pierce deep into every science and to enquire the nature of every substance. 'The materials of science, in fact', writes William K Wimsatt, 'and the history of scientific words in English for the past century and a half provided him [Johnson] with perhaps his main opportunity for illustrating the metaphoric growth of meaning' (*Philosophic Words*). In relation to The Vision, the chosen genre of allegory, allows science to be imported into the text in a most ingenious way. Taking the form of a dream, this literary piece is also a Newtonian vision that is just as much about the physical phenomena of pictures propagated by motions along the fibres of the optick nerves into the brain as about their imaginative reconstruction in a dream. 'A dream is supposed natural, a vision miraculous; but they are confounded' is how Johnson articulates the meaning of sense 4 of 'vision' in *The Dictionary*. And with imagination perpetually on the wings, his poetic mind is put in motion on a journey with no frontiers in The Vision. The suspended vista of abstracted elementary solid forms renders the whole an atmosphere of reverie that betrays the drama of the self and the depth of Johnson's searching creative mind. Rigorously tied up to the landscape, yet detached and unaware of the world around, Theodore's dream is a vision from within. The topographical configurations, delineated in a unified system of geometrical patterns, liberate the visual elements, unleashing their potency for multiple interpretations. And as the finiteness of nature vanishes in 'the discernible mist', proceeding from one truth to another, independent and unconnected sentiments flash upon the mind in quick succession to form a whole, because in Johnson's words 'to connect distant propositions by regular consequences is the great prerogative of man' (*Rambler* 158).

Today The Vision is known as Johnson's first allegorical writing or a little allegory that carries the usual moral concept of his writings. Mentioned often is the fact that it was produced by Johnson in one night with his proverbial speed together with The Preface to *The Preceptor*. This opinion has solidified on the critical arena but it needs to be reviewed as The Vision is a composition of a distinct kind that requires careful consideration that is void of the ascribed rashness of writing. It must be remembered that in the mid-eighteenth century science was post-Newtonian science of corporeal matter and the study of the mind with its cognitive power and metaphysical came under close scrutiny.

It is suggested that in The Vision Johnson weaves concepts of naked science with resourceful imagination and ingenious artistic dexterity - its meticulous design has Bacon's approach to detail in structure while the allusions to space, mass, colour and light are of Newtonian magnitude. First, Johnson always professed that writing should inform the reader and the task of the writer was to popularize knowledge in an accessible form. Next, The Vision was written in the mid-eighteenth century at the time when the influence of Bacon and Newton was strongly felt in all disciplines, and Johnson expressed his admiration for them on many occasions.

B. Analysis of *The Vision*

The influence of Francis Bacon (1561-1626) and Isaac Newton (1642-1727)

Richard Schwartz's book Samuel Johnson and the New Science (1971) still remains the only authority on the subject of Johnson's scientific thought and his positive views of the Baconian scientific tradition, for which he provides a wealth of referential evidence. Schwartz noted that science was the core of our understanding of the spirit of the age of Johnson and was adamant that 'the English tradition of science and scientific ideology – to which the empirical methodology is central' is a fact that was self-evident to Voltaire. In his Preliminary Discourse to the *Encyclopaedia* of Diderot, D'Alembert declares British science the 'world model' and pays tribute to Newton for giving 'philosophy a form which apparently it is to keep'; to Locke for reducing physics to what it really ought to be: the experimental physics of the soul'; and to Bacon, the 'immortal Chancellor', who 'prepared from afar the light which gradually, by imperceptible degrees, would illuminate the world'. According to the great French mathematician, Bacon, Newton and Locke were towering above all those who were prepared to follow the torch of truth. Schwartz gave numerous examples confirming Bacon's influence on Johnson's own outlook which affirmed the proposition that if we were to learn the constituent characteristics of Johnson's methodology, we should be better equipped to re-examine his works from a new critical perspective that included his positive attitude to science, his open response to a diversity of ideas and his encouragement of applied science and the arts.

W K Wimsatt also noted the great number of references to Bacon's works in *The Rambler*, observing that only from Bacon's *Natural History*, 'in Johnson's eyes the parent and sufficient authority for English philosophic diction', Johnson had used some 75 illustrations in these essays. Furthermore, Wimsatt's study of about 380 *Rambler* philosophic words and their illustrative quotations in *The Dictionary* had shown Bacon to be 'the single author most often quoted' (*Philosophic Words*), and this fact alone deserves greater attention. Also, reminiscences of his contemporaries point to Johnson's interest in Bacon and Newton. In Life, Boswell, for example, recollected that in 1760 in the house of Mrs Cholmondeley during a conversation with Pere Boscovitch, the Jesuit astronomer, he heard Johnson 'maintain the superiority of Sir Isaac Newton over all foreign philosophers'. He was of the opinion that intellectual pre-eminence was the highest superiority bestowed upon humankind and had unreserved admiration for Newton's power of mind. Another time, in a critical remark on the merits of a poem by David Mallet who praised the superiority of the ancient times, Johnson was categorical that 'there is now a great deal more learning in the world than there was formerly; for it is universally diffused', but there may now be 'no man who knows as much Greek and Latin as Bentley; and no man who knows as much mathematics as Newton'; though there may be 'many more men who know Greek and Latin, and who know mathematics'. Wimsatt observed that to the apparent influence of Bacon, Johnson's distinctly creative and progressive style was often tinged with 'all the mixtures of colorifick radiance' from Newton's *Opticks*. Calling it 'one of the purest fountainheads from the stream of scientific ideas and diction', Wimsatt traced its influence in many of Johnson's periodical essays. But the way in which Johnson engaged in a metaphoric transfer of science concepts in The Vision was not noted.

That Johnson thought highly of Bacon and Newton is undisputable. In his reflection on the merit of academic life and in his defence of Cambridge and Oxford as 'celebrated seats' of learning, Johnson put across one 'very powerful incentive for learning' there, that being the 'Genius of the place'. This he defined as

> A sort of inspiring deity which every youth of quick sensibility and ingenious disposition creates to himself, by reflecting, that he is placed under those venerable walls, where a Hooker and a Hammond, a Bacon and a Newton, once pursued the same course of science, and from whence they soared to the most elevated heights, of literary fame (*The Idler* 33).

Johnson's view of Bacon and Newton is a resounding confirmation of his regard for their works and a venerable recognition of their genius. The true Genius for Johnson is 'a mind of large general powers'; and undoubtedly Bacon's lofty eloquence, wide learning, comprehensive views, and bold predictions made men listen attentively to what he had to say. For him, Bacon's writings, from ethical and political to scientific, historical and legal, were 'the observations of a strong mind operate operating upon life' which confirms the importance he placed upon the breadth of the philosopher's knowledge, 'scarcely attained by any other man'. But more importantly, they were the result of a comprehensive study of mankind based on observation and personal experience, 'for who can teach an art with so great authority, as he that has practiced it with undisputed success?'. Welcoming Bacon's vast embrace and his directions concerning the interpretation of nature, Johnson rejected the narrow compass of the singular outlook which he identified with the disjointed and fragmented; and the influence of Bacon's fifty-eight essays can be traced in Johnson's own essays on human nature.

Further, the Newtonian ideas of universality and infinite diversity found also expression in eighteenth-century aesthetics. The attempt of isolating the 'particular' as being inherently beautiful was replaced by another line of beauty – that of Newton's pyramidal form – solid and indestructible as much as enigmatic. The tension is best expressed by William Hogarth (1697-1764) who in *The Analysis of Beauty* (1753) chose a serpentine line woven round a pyramid for the front cover. Hogarth rejected 'strong prejudices in favour of straight lines, as constituting true beauty in human form' and was critical of the French painters who 'avoided the serpentine line in all their pictures', and praised Rubens for making 'use of a large flowing line'. Hogarth's serpentine line is symbolic of Newton's infinite variety of bulk in motion, converging lines and retiring shades, the obliquity of planes, grading colours and effulgent light (on Hogarth's admiration for Newton, see his painting 'The Indian Emperor or The Conquest of Mexico' of 1732 where the bust of Newton is prominently featured. Indeed, the colours of Newton's rainbow, with its promise of peace and reconciliation after the storm, the flash of the diamond, the hues of the prism and the rings of the soap-bubble were the very things curious early to mid-eighteenth-century scientists observed in the telescope. 'It has been discovered by Sir Isaac Newton, that the distinct and primogenial colours are only seven', Johnson reflected, affirming that every eye can witness that 'from various mixtures in various propositions, infinite diversifications of tints may be produced' (*The Adventurer* 95). Then he hastens to add that the same can be observed with human nature if we were to analyse the human mind. The mid-eighteenth century was enthralled by Newton's idea of colour being equated with light, 'a philosophical idea, when we consider the various colours to be different sensations, exited in use by the refracted rays of light, reflected on our eyes in a different manner' (*The Dictionary*). Thus the poetry of Alexander Pope (1688-1744), Richard Savage (1697-1743) James Thomson (1700-1748), David Mallet (1705-1765) amongst others bathed in the effulgence of light darting across the sky, splitting the ray into a rainbow of colours. 'An object, however small in itself, if placed near to the eye, will engross all the rays of light', Johnson remarked in *Rambler* 106, and noted that by analogy, 'a transaction, however trivial, swells into importance, when it presses immediately on our attention'. This is how he effortlessly succeeds in applying a science concept to a matter more mundane and ordinary.

Since the time of Johnson's work on *The Dictionary* coincides with his first exposure to the works of Bacon by which he was greatly influenced, it is possible that Bacon's concept of 'design' and 'plan' are fully operational in The Vision – the most creative of Johnson's literary writings. However, its meticulous plan may have Bacon's approach to detail in structure, but his allusions to space, mass, colour and light are of Newtonian magnitude. The imagery of 'birds of light' singing in the trees as 'the glances of the morning darted' upon the hermit Theodore in The Vision is Johnson's most ingenious poetical allusion of Newton's concept of colour and light.

A poet of physical and human Nature
It is in The Vision where Johnson's artistic imagination reaches its peak and where he clearly demonstrates that he shared truly the sensibility of his age. The suspended vista of abstracted elementary solid forms renders the whole an atmosphere of reverie that betrays the drama of the self and the depth of Johnson's searching and sensitive mind. Rigorously tied up to the landscape, yet detached and unaware of the world around, Theodore's dream is a vision from within. The topographical configurations, delineated in a unified system of geometrical patterns, liberate the visual elements, unleashing their potency for multiple interpretations. As the finiteness of nature vanishes in 'the discernible mist', proceeding from one truth to another, independent and unconnected sentiments flash upon the mind in quick succession because 'to connect distant propositions by regular consequences in the great prerogative of man' (*Rambler* 158). Marking initially the compass of the whole, by means of a hierarchical division and sub-division of a pyramid, Johnson proceeds to create the frame of the 'scale of human existence' – the four phases of human life, from childhood to youth and maturity to old age. Each operational power is designated a dominion by virtue of its subordinate strength, starting from the personified figure of Innocence and proceeding to Education, thereon to the province of Reason, followed by that of the most superior of all four, Religion. In each of the four labelled dominions Johnson marks by gradation the presence of various personified Appetites and Passions acting as forces within human nature.

The design consisting of inclined planes –uneven and angular, is more than a strict replica of Bacon's meticulous hierarchical pyramid of a seemingly solid pyramidal figure with plain triangular sides. It is also Newtonian in concept - irregular, infinite and unresolved, it reminds one of 'the cone of being' where the base is at an infinite distance from the top. The protagonist of the story, the hermit Theodore, trembled at the formidable sight of the imaginary mountain, 'higher than Teneriffe, to the summit of which the human eye could never reach'; and when tired of 'gazing upon its height', he turned his eyes 'towards its foot' only to find to his amazement that it was 'without foundation, and placed inconceivably in emptiness and darkness'. If we trace the contours of Johnson's scale of existence in The Vision, from the emptiness of the bottomless base, through to the wide plane with its smooth surface and follow up the ever narrowing two lines of the path to where they merge into a point that is invisible in the discernible mist, is it not the shape of a cone that Johnson is outlining? The seemingly firm and stable surface of the earth is juxtaposed with interrelations of immobility and movement, of chaos and order; the massive forms, rounded and irregular are opposed to the dynamic horizontal and vertical lines that are calmed by the trees and the sloping lines – they all impart depth to the landscape and produce the visual impression of an elongated wedge. Our eyes travel from the imagery of the steep, fractured rocks, ruddy in the light and grey in the shadows, to the gently sloping planes with delicate surface markings under a soft light. As the cliffs with their upright clefts merge with the organic shapes of the towering trees and dissipate beyond the void of the sky, the vision of nature becomes one of a detached presence, inviting no action, only discernment of the momentary and the timeless.

The picture forms a dense network and acquires a third dimension – that of depth. More than that, the massif of the mountain develops the effect of a curving space as if the landscape is painted on a convex, spherical surface. The reader is compelled by the ultimate balance of opposing and unstable forces operating upon human nature, each one of them an embodiment of a complex set of ideas, nonetheless representing only a small chain in the definitive whole. And the Mountain of Existence, with its inscrutable tracts, becomes a pictorial abstraction of universal magnitude and a vivid illustration of Johnson's firm belief in the imperfectability of human nature, with its incessant wants anchored in time – temporal, vain and insatiable.

Johnson's Mountain of Existence

In choosing the dynamics of Newtonian physics and applying his simplicity of logic and inference, Johnson succeeds in deducing his own operating principles of the universal traits of human nature – from China to Peru, from the dawn of humankind to present day. It is a formidable imaginary sight of a multitude of both sexes, climbing up the Mountain of Existence, constantly besieged by various desires and enchained by Habits, at no one time capable of achieving and sustaining equilibrium in their present state on earth. Johnson uses the Newtonian attributes of force as a vector quality, its size and directions, and the knowledge that its continuous application causes a body to gain or lose velocity to recreate endless scenes of human warfare with formidable creative stride. The reader follows eagerly the perpetual motion of the animated figures of Habits. 'Bad' Habits remain 'never at a stand' and are 'continually growing or decreasing' in 'bulk', they join up forces with Appetites or Passion and succeed in changing the direction of the wayfarers to their detriment. 'Good' Habits, on the other hand, are seen to 'glide' along with no friction from opposing forces 'in the road of Happiness' in front of the travellers who are distinguished with their 'uniformity of march'. There is no evidence of any conflicting forces in the province of Innocence for that speck of time referring to the 'childhood' of humankind. Alas, this is only a brief moment in the passage of time, marked otherwise by the turbulent action of reactionary forces.

Newton's laws of universal gravitation with the concepts of motion, force, mass and change of direction are related to the theme of resistance and forceful subjugation to 'bad' habits; or by inference on a larger scale to the enslavement of the human spirit during man's temporal earthly existence, the subjugation of individuals or whole nations by 'supreme powers'. It appears that when the 'action' force of Education meets with the 'reaction' force of Appetites, no change of direction occurs; but as soon as 'bad' Habits join in, their size reaches gigantic proportions and leads to a change of the travellers' direction. Following anxiously the route of the wayfarers upon the curvy crust of the Earth where the force of gravity is always present, it is evident that their forward motion is constantly subjected to resistant forces. We witness the constant subjection of the travellers to the forces of Appetites, Passions, Pride and Ambition, joined by the bulky mass of Habits continually increasing or decreasing in size. It transpires that equilibrium in the province of Reason is best maintained when the resistant forces are kept apart so 'they counteracted one another' and 'the path of Reason was best followed, when a Passion was called to one side, and an Appetite to the other'. In the domain of Religion, a balance is kept best when 'good' Habits, stand in the middle of the travellers' passage, vigorously supporting' them and 'driving their Appetites and Passions' on either side.

Johnson uses both attributes of the Newtonian concept of 'force' as a vector of quantity, that is its size and its direction; as well as the knowledge that the continuous application of a 'force' to a body causes it to gain or lose velocity. Thus, the action of the augmented force of Habits upon the voyagers accelerates their abrupt and precipitous motion and they are forced to wander off in various directions along the winding mountainous road. The whole picture resembles a tug of war in a magnificently staged conflict. The reader travels along the steep with the wayfarers only to witness time and time again the secret ambush by 'bad' Habits that seize their victims 'in the regions of Desire'. As they shackle them with chains that could never be broken, they drag them along as slaves 'in the caverns of Despair', or engulf them in the retreats of tyrants where neither Hope nor Fear could enter. A true master of human nature, Johnson observes that 'to walk with circumspection and steadiness in the right path, at an equal distance between the extremes of error', is a difficult task for human beings to endeavour at any one time.

The imaginary design is aided by the Newtonian concept of extension of matter, resulting in meticulous coordination of the presented detail. Whereas there are no visible forces in the first domain of Innocence, Appetites and Habits appear to be in operation in the domain of Education. These are joined by Passions in the third province, that of Reason, where there are additionally marked extensions to Appetites and Passions, Lust to the former and Vanity to the latter. By further extensions, are added the regions of Desire and Despair, the bower of Content and Pride and the side tracks of Ambition, Avarice, Intemperance, Indolence and Melancholy. In The Dictionary, 'extension n.s.' is defined as 'the act of being extended' and is illustrated with a quotation by Locke that reads: 'By this idea of solidity is the extension of body distinguished from the extension of space...'. The wealth of the chosen vocabulary and the abundance of personifications, no doubt, contribute to the rich texture of meaning which affords many levels of interpretation – from the general to the deeply philosophical relating to the brutal and restless nature of man or to the turbulent history of civilizations, steeped in blood and submerged in slavery and subjugation.

Johnson also applies Newton's concept of fluxions that is the differential calculus which Newton had described as the 'method of fluxions' in *The Principia Mathematica* of 1687 whereby a variable quantity x , depending on time is called a fluent, and its rate of change with time is said to be the fluxion of the fluent. The Newtonian notion is used to describe the change of state of the hermit Theodore who after forty-eight years 'passed in forgetfulness of all mortal care' in procurement of the basic necessities of life, experiences the sudden awakening of 'a desire' to climb the rock overhanging his cell, and propelled by its inner impulse which proves insatiable, he sets off up the mountainous path. The provisions pull him down and the sand slides 'from beneath his feet' as 'the declivities grew more precipitous'. Theodore's journey can be expressed as a jagged line generated by a point moving along an inclined plane where the force of gravity is continually weighing him down, and together with the friction of the sand, opposes the velocity of his upward stride. The speed of his ascent gradually decreases until 'at last, fainting with labour', he arrives at a small horizontal plain that marks the end of the slope and denotes an equilibrium of forces – and also an end to his temporal desire. The declivities, as a tangent to a slope, represent the varying degrees of elevation of Theodore's desire where the slope symbolizes the curving crust of the earth; and since knowing the slope of the tangent means knowing the slope of the curve, the declivities can be perceived as gradients measuring the rate of change, a concept of Newtonian physics that is used ingeniously by Johnson.

Following anxiously the route of the wayfarers climbing up the craggy winding path, it becomes evident that all their forward motion is persistently retarded by resistant forces. The gradient of the slope of the precipitous declivities in the topographical configuration of the Mountain of Existence clearly denotes the gradual increase in the rate of change of human desires. The meticulous design reveals that as humans advance from childhood to youth and then to middle age their Appetites and Passions take a more 'extensive range'; it also affirms Johnson's view that desires are an inherent trait in human nature and 'will be always raging'.

The tempo of the entire composition changes – the gentle flowery green mass at the bottom that is suggestive of pastoral movement is succeeded by the slow rhythm of ascent which intensifies into a crescendo in the middle where the planes rise higher and higher, and slows down gradually – leaving a clear impression of the mountain receding endlessly into the distance. In aerial perspective form foreground to horizon, each stage of life is defined as a step in an evolving process – that of the finiteness of human life.

The vector of Time as a marker of life
More than that, the concepts of the 'finite' and 'infinite' are closely linked with Newtonian science at the time, permitting to make sense of other factors in the field of politics, economics, philosophy, literature and the arts. In The Vision, Johnson engages these concepts philosophically as well as aesthetically

in his portrayal of the Mountain of Existence. The area between the flowery bottom of the mountain right up to its highest visible part marks the temporal human existence – the 'finite'; whereas the suggested projection of the line into the 'mist' with 'the temple of Happiness' denotes the eternal – the infinite and enigmatic. Human life is portrayed as a natural progression from childhood to manhood to old age; therefore 'no man can taste the fruits of autumn while he is delighting his scent with the flowers of spring'. The movement of the year from spring to winter is related to the idea of mortality, inevitable progressive path of birth, maturation, degeneration and decay.

To denote 'time' in The Vision Johnson employs symbolic imagery that marks the stages of human life. The initial gentle rise of the Mountain of Existence, 'overspread with flowers' conjures up an image of spring, and signifies the carefree time of childhood, the age of innocence, fleeting by nature though, thus temporal; the uneven configuration of its middle part, rising in steepness by gradation, and intercepted by 'crags' and 'precipices' is suggestive of the 'vicissitudes of life' that characterize the years of youth and maturity where the imagery of trees loaded with ripe fruits hanging from the branches relates to the seasons of summer and signifies existing temptations and although with a longer life span than flowers, the fruits are still perishable, still of temporal, 'finite' nature. Finally the discernible top of the mountain marks the end of the scale of earthly existence and is depicted only by 'a few hardy evergreens' denoting longevity and endurance whereas the sparse vegetation and lack of choice in the natural phenomena implies also lack of choice in the latter years of human life; the sight of the trees that 'did not give much pleasure to the sight or smell' may well signify diminishing physical abilities and unlike the tantalizing vitality of the previous stages, the 'generally barren' configuration of the landscape at the top of the mountain speaks of the decay and decrepitude of old age, still temporal, still finite in nature.

Johnson's views of the temporal nature of life is rooted in his understanding of the concept of the 'finite', in relation to the eternal nature of the Universe, the 'infinite'. Human life is perceived as evolution, a natural progression from childhood to manhood to old age; therefore 'no man can taste the fruits of autumn while he is delighting his scent with the flowers of spring'. In *The Dictionary*, 'time' is defined as 'the measure of duration' and is supported with an illustrative quotation from Ecclesiastes: 'To everything there is a season, and a time to every purpose'.

Further still, watching the travellers upon the surface of the earth, it is feasible to accept that they represent an abstraction of the 'infinite' series of those forgotten multitudes of former ages, from the dawn of humankind to the present day. In Preface to *The Preceptor*, Johnson wrote:

> History lays open to you all Countries, Times and Transactions and makes you in a Manner an Eye-Witness to the astonishing Changes and Resolutions that have from time to time happened in the Worlds – we carry ourselves to the first Original of Things and enter upon a new kind of Experience.

Thus, by inference or analogy The Vision becomes 'a representation of things, close, distance and ancient' since by abstracting stable truths, Johnson probes to the limits of the world as we know it.

The eternal presence in The Vision

At the final scene, Johnson creates atmospheric suspense through the image of the hopeless wanderer, tortured by Melancholy and consigned to the cruelty of Despair, with the chains of Habit riveted for ever; whereas the captives of Indolence struck by Discontent, with Sadness, hovering round their shades, crawl on reluctantly in gloom 'till they arrived at the depth of the recess, varied with poppies and nightshade'.

But as light struggles with darkness, the 'glances of the morning' sun dart in, giving rise to colour, and sound is borne in the air by the song of the birds. The imagery of 'birds of light' singing in the trees as 'the glances of the morning darted' upon the hermit is Johnson's most ingenious poetical allusion of Newton's concept of colour and light. As in a camera obscura, the outer world is projected onto the inner screen of the eye and light and vision proceed as rays in space – extended, entwined with the conception of space – moral space and spiritual light, perspective space and geometrical light.

A marriage of outer and inner light forges a link between the objects of the world and the soul and acts as a mediator between man and a dark, cavernous world. A link is formed, and as the message passes into the mind' eye, it crafts images based on experience and imagination.

The sudden shooting light and its unsettling splendour of glimmerings dissolve the story that refuses to close.

Innovative in design, The Vision is a revelation of Johnson's creative mind. In seeking the active participation of the reader in deciphering the symbolic nature of purely visual elements, The Vision is an experience of 'awakened seeing'. The ideas are neither fixed nor limited, but malleable and expansive and the language stripped from the ballast of adorned literary content reveals the unchanging in art.

THE VISION OF THEODORE, THE HERMIT OF TENERIFFE, FOUND IN HIS CELL 1748

*Prelude to The Vision of Theodore,
by Svetlan Stefanov*

Son of Perseverance, whoever thou art, whose curiosity has led thee hither, read and be wise.

The Hermit in his cell

He that now calls upon thee is Theodore, the Hermit of Teneriffe, who in the fifty-seventh year of his retreat left this instruction to mankind, lest his solitary hours should be spent in vain.

I was once what thou art now, a groveller on the earth, and a gazer at the Sky; I trafficked and heaped wealth together, I loved and was favoured, I wore the robe of honour and heard the musick of adulation: I was ambitious, and rose to greatness: I was unhappy, and retired. I sought for some time what I at length found here, a place where all real wants might be easily supplied, and where I might not be under the necessity of purchasing the assistance of men by the toleration of their follies. Here I saw fruits and herbs and water, and here determined to wait the hand of death, which I hope, when at last it comes, will fall lightly upon me.

Forty-eight years had I now passed in forgetfulness of all mortal cares, and without any inclination to wander farther than the necessity of procuring sustenance required; but as I stood one day beholding the rock that overhangs my cell, I found in myself a desire to climb it; and when I was on its top, was in the same manner determined to scale the next, till by degrees I conceived a wish to view the summit of the mountain, at the foot of which I had so long resided.

This motion of my thoughts I endeavoured to suppress, not because it appeared criminal, but because it was new; and all change not evidently for the better, alarms a mind taught by experience to distrust itself. I was often afraid that my heart was deceiving me, that my impatience of confinement arose from some earthly passion, and that my ardour to survey the works of nature was only a hidden longing to mingle once again in the scenes of life.

I therefore endeavoured to settle my thoughts into their former state, but found their distraction every day greater.

I was always reproaching myself with the want of happiness within my reach, and at last began to question whether it was not laziness rather than caution that restrained me from climbing to the summit of Teneriffe.

I rose therefore before the day, and began my journey up the steep of the mountain; but I had not advanced far, old as I was and burdened with provisions, when the day began to shine upon me; the declivities grew more precipitous, and the sand slided from beneath my feet; at last, fainting with labour, I arrived at a small plain almost enclosed by rocks, and open only to the east.

The rocks of Teneriffe

I sat down to rest

I sat down to rest awhile, in full persuasion, that when I had recovered my strength I should proceed on my design; but when once I had tasted ease, I found many reasons against disturbing it. The branches spread a shade over my head, and the gales of spring wafted odours to my bosom.

As I sat thus, forming alternately excuses for delay, and resolutions to go forward, an irresistible heaviness suddenly surprised me; I laid my head upon the bank, and resigned myself to sleep: when methought I heard the sound as of the flight of eagles, and a being of more than human dignity stood before me.

While I was deliberating how to address him, he took me by the hand with an air of kindness, and asked me solemnly, but without severity, "Theodore, whither art thou going?" "I am climbing," answered I, "to the top of the mountain, to enjoy a more extensive prospect of the works of nature."

"Attend first," said he, "to the prospect which this place affords, and what thou dost not understand I will explain. I am one of the benevolent beings who watch over the children of the dust, to preserve them from those evils which will not ultimately terminate in good, and which they do not, by their own faults, bring upon themselves. Look round therefore without fear: observe, contemplate, and be instructed."

Encouraged by this assurance, I looked and beheld a mountain higher than Teneriffe, to the summit of which the human eye could never reach: when I had tired myself with gazing upon its height, I turned my eyes towards its foot, which I could easily discover, but was amazed to find it without foundation, and placed inconceivably in emptiness and darkness.

Thus I stood terrified and confused; above were tracks inscrutable, and below was total vacuity. But my protector, with a voice of admonition, cried out, "Theodore, be not affrighted, but raise thy eyes again; the Mountain of Existence is before thee, survey it and be wise."

I then looked with more deliberate attention, and observed the bottom of the mountain to be of gentle rise, and overspread with flowers; the middle to be more steep, embarrassed with crags, and interrupted by precipices, over which hung branches loaded with fruits, and among which were scattered palaces and bowers. The tracts which my eye could reach nearest the top were generally barren; but there were among the clefts of the rocks a few hardy evergreens, which though they did not give much pleasure to the sight or smell, yet seemed to cheer the labour and facilitate the steps of those who were clambering among them.

I heard the sound as of the flight of eagles

The Mountain of Existence

Then, beginning to examine more minutely the different parts, I observed at a great distance a multitude of both sexes issuing into view from the bottom of the mountain. Their first actions I could not accurately discern; but, as they every moment approached nearer, I found that they amused themselves with gathering flowers under the superintendence of a modest virgin in a white robe, who seemed not over solicitous to confine them to any settled pace or certain track; for she knew that the whole ground was smooth and solid, and that they could not easily be hurt or bewildered. When, as it often happened, they plucked a thistle for a flower, Innocence, so was she called, would smile at the mistake. Happy, said I, are they who are under so gentle a government, and yet are safe.

But I had no opportunity to dwell long on the consideration of their felicity; for I found that Innocence continued her attendance but a little way, and seemed to consider only the flowery bottom of the mountain as her proper province.

Those whom she abandoned scarcely knew that they were left, before they perceived themselves in the hands of Education, a nymph more severe in her aspect, and imperious in her commands, who confined them to certain paths, in their opinion too narrow and too rough. These they were continually solicited to leave by Appetite, whom Education could never fright away, though she sometimes awed her to such timidity, that the effects of her presence were scarcely perceptible.

Some went back to the first part of the mountain, and seemed desirous of continuing busied in plucking flowers, but were no longer guarded by Innocence; and such as Education could not force back, proceeded up the mountain by some miry road, in which they were seldom seen, and scarcely ever regarded.

As Education led her troop up the mountain, nothing was more observable than that she was frequently giving them cautions to beware of Habits; and was calling out to one or another at every step, that a Habit was insnaring them; that they would be under the dominion of Habit before they perceived their danger; and that those whom Habit should once subdue, had little hope of regaining their liberty.

In the Path of Education

Of this caution, so frequently repeated, I was very solicitous to know the reason, when my protector directed my regard to a troop of pygmies, which appeared to walk silently before those that were climbing the mountain, and each to smooth the way before her follower. I found that I had missed the notice of them before, both because they were so minute as not easily to be discerned, and because they grew every moment nearer their colour to the objects with which they were surrounded. As the followers of Education did not appear to be sensible of the presence of these dangerous associates, or, ridiculing their diminutive size, did not think it possible that human beings should ever be brought into subjection by such feeble enemies, they generally heard her precepts of vigilance with wonder: and, when they thought her eye withdrawn, treated them with contempt. Nor could I myself think her cautions so necessary as her frequent inculcations seemed to suppose, till I observed that each of these petty beings held secretly a chain in her hand, with which she prepared to bind those whom she found within her power. Yet these Habits under the eye of Education went quietly forward, and seemed very little to increase in bulk or strength; for though they were always willing to join with Appetite, yet when Education kept them apart from her, they would very punctually obey command, and make the narrow roads in which they were confined easier, and smoother.

It was observable, that their stature was never at a stand, but continually growing or decreasing, yet not always in the same proportions: nor could I forbear to express my admiration, when I saw in how much less time they generally gained than lost bulk. Though they grew slowly in the road of Education, it might however be perceived that they grew; but if they once deviated at the call of Appetite, their stature soon became gigantick; and their strength was such, that Education pointed out to her tribe many that were led in chains by them, whom she could never more rescue from their slavery. She pointed them out, but with little effect; for all her pupils appeared confident of their own superiority to the strongest Habit, and some seemed in secret to regret that they were hindered from following the triumph of Appetite.

It was the peculiar artifice of Habit not to suffer her power to be felt at first. Those whom she led, she had the address of appearing only to attend, but was continually doubling her chains upon her companions; which were so slender in themselves, and so silently fastened, that while the attention was engaged by other objects, they were not easily perceived. Each link grew tighter as it had been longer worn; and when by continual additions they became so heavy as to be felt, they were very frequently too strong to be broken.

When Education had proceeded in this manner to the part of the mountain where the declivity began to grow craggy, she resigned her charge to two powers of superiour aspect. The meaner of them appeared capable of presiding in senates, or governing nations, and yet watched the steps of the other with the most anxious attention, and was visibly confounded and perplexed if ever she suffered her regard to be drawn away.

The other seemed to approve her submission as pleasing, but with such a condescension as plainly shewed that she claimed it as due; and indeed so great was her dignity and sweetness, that he who would not reverence, must not behold her.

Temptations

"Theodore," said my protector, "be fearless, and be wise; approach these powers, whose dominion extends to all the remaining part of the Mountain of Existence." I trembled, and ventured to address the inferiour nymph, whose eyes, though piercing and awful, I was not able to sustain. "Bright Power," said I, "by whatever name it is lawful to address thee, tell me, thou who presidest here, on what condition thy protection will be granted?" "It will he granted," said she, "only to obedience. I am Reason, of all subordinate beings the noblest and the greatest; who, if thou wilt receive my laws, will reward thee like the rest of my votaries, by conducting thee to Religion." Charmed by her voice and aspect, I professed my readiness to follow her. She then presented me to her mistress, who looked upon me with tenderness. I bowed before her, and she smiled.

Reason, the noblest and the greatest

When Education delivered up those for whose happiness she had been so long solicitous, she seemed to expect that they should express some gratitude for her care, or some regret at the loss of that protection which she had hitherto afforded them. But it was easy to discover, by the alacrity which broke out at her departure, that her presence had been long displeasing, and that she had been teaching those who felt in themselves no want of instruction. They all agreed in rejoicing that they should no longer be subject to her caprices, or disturbed by her documents, but should be now under the direction only of Reason, to whom they made no doubt of being able to recommend themselves by a steady adherence to all her precepts. Reason counselled them, at their first entrance upon her province, to enlist themselves among the votaries of Religion; and informed them, that if they trusted to her alone, they would find the same fate with her other admirers, whom she had not been able to secure against Appetites and Passions and who, having been seized by Habits in the regions of Desire, had been dragged away to the caverns of Despair. Her admonition was vain, the greater number declared against any other direction, and doubted not but by her superintendency they should climb with safety up the Mountain of Existence. "My power," said Reason, "is to advise, not to compel; I have already told you the danger of your choice. The path seems now plain and even, but there are asperities and pitfalls, over which Religion only can conduct you. Look upwards, and you perceive a mist before you settled upon the highest visible part of the mountain; a mist by which my prospect is terminated, and which is pierced only by the eyes of Religion. Beyond it are the temples of Happiness, in which those who climb the precipice by her direction, after the toil of their pilgrimage, repose for ever. I know not the way, and therefore can only conduct you to a better guide. Pride has sometimes reproached me with the narrowness of my view, but, when she endeavoured to extend it, could only shew me, below the mist, the bowers of Content; even they vanished as I fixed my eyes upon them; and those whom she persuaded to travel towards them were enchained by Habits, and ingulfed by Despair, a cruel tyrant, whose caverns are beyond the darkness on the right side and on the left, from whose prisons none can escape, and whom I cannot teach you to avoid."

Religion

Such was the declaration of Reason to those who demanded her protection. Some that recollected the dictates of Education, finding them now seconded by another authority, submitted with reluctance to the strict decree, and engaged themselves among the followers of Religion, who were distinguished by the uniformity of their march, though many of them were women, and by their continual endeavours to move upwards, without appearing to regard the prospects which at every step courted their attention.

All those who determined to follow either Reason or Religion, were continually importuned to forsake the road, sometimes by Passions, and sometimes by Appetites, of whom both had reason to boast the success of their artifices; for so many were drawn into bypaths, that any way was more populous than the right. The attacks of the Appetites were more impetuous, those of the Passions longer continued. The Appetites turned their followers directly from the true way; but the Passions marched at first in a path nearly in the same direction with that of Reason and Religion, but deviated by slow degrees, till at last they entirely changed their course. Appetite drew aside the dull, and Passion the sprightly. Of the Appetites, Lust was the strongest; and of the Passions, Vanity. The most powerful assault was to be feared, when a Passion and an Appetite joined their enticements; and the path of Reason was best followed, when a Passion called to one side, and an Appetite to the other.

These seducers had the greatest success upon the followers of Reason, over whom they scarcely ever failed to prevail, except when they counteracted one another. They had not the same triumphs over the votaries of Religion; for though they were often led aside for a time, Religion commonly recalled them by her emissary Conscience, before Habit had time to enchain them. But they that professed to obey Reason, if once they forsook her, seldom returned; for she had no messenger to summon them but Pride, who generally betrayed her confidence, and employed all her skill to support Passion; and if ever she did her duty, was found unable to prevail, if Habit had interposed.

I soon found that the great danger to the followers of Religion was only from Habit; every other power was easily resisted, nor did they find any difficulty, when they inadvertently quitted her, to find her again by the direction of Conscience, unless they had given time to Habit to draw her chain behind them, and bar up the way by which they had wandered. Of some of those, the condition was justly to be pitied, who turned at every call of Conscience, and tried, but without effect, to burst the chains of Habit: saw Religion walking forward at a distance, saw her with reverence, and longed to join her; but were, whenever they approached her, withheld by Habit, and languished in sordid bondage, which they could not escape, though they scorned and hated it.

The bondage of Habits

It was evident that the Habits were so far from growing weaker by these repeated contests, that if they were not totally overcome, every struggle enlarged their bulk and increased their strength; and a Habit opposed and victorious was more than twice as strong as before the contest. The manner in which those who were weary of their tyranny endeavoured to escape from them, appeared by the event to be generally wrong; they tried to loose their chains one by one, and to retreat by the same degrees as they advanced; but before the deliverance was completed, Habit always threw new chains upon her fugitive; nor did any escape her but those who, by an effort sudden and violent, burst their shackles at once, and left her at a distance; and even of these, many rushing too precipitately forward, and hindered by their terrours from stopping where they were safe, were fatigued with their own vehemence, and resigned themselves again to that power from whom an escape must be so dearly bought, and whose tyranny was little felt, except when it was resisted.

Some however there always were, who when they found Habit prevailing over them, called upon Reason or Religion for assistance; each of them willingly came to the succour of her suppliant, but neither with the same strength, nor the same success. Habit, insolent with her power, would often presume to parley with Reason, and offer to loose some of her chains if the rest might remain.

To this Reason, who was never certain of victory, frequently consented, but always found her concession destructive, and saw the captive led away by Habit to his former slavery.

Religion never submitted to treaty, but held out her hand with certainty of conquest; and if the captive to whom she gave it did not quit his hold, always led him away in triumph, and placed him in the direct path to the Temple of Happiness, where Reason never failed to congratulate his deliverance, and encourage his adherence to that power to whose timely succour he was indebted for it.

The Road of Happiness

When the traveller was again placed in the road of Happiness, I saw Habit again gliding before him, but reduced to the stature of a dwarf, without strength and without activity; but when the Passions or Appetites, which had before seduced him, made their approach, Habit would on a sudden start into size, and with unexpected violence push him towards them. The wretch, thus impelled on one side, and allured on the other, too frequently quitted the road of Happiness, to which, after his second deviation from it, he rarely returned: but, by a timely call upon Religion, the force of Habit was eluded, her attacks grew fainter, and at last her correspondence with the enemy was entirely destroyed. She then began to employ those restless faculties in compliance with the power which she could not overcome; and as she grew again in stature and in strength, cleared away the asperities of the Road to Happiness.

From this road I could not easily withdraw my attention, because all who travelled it appeared cheerful and satisfied; and the farther they proceeded, the greater appeared their alacrity, and the stronger their conviction of the wisdom of their guide. Some, who had never deviated but by short excursions, had Habit in the middle of their passage vigorously supporting them, and driving off their Appetites and Passions which attempted to interrupt their progress. Others, who had entered this road late, or had long forsaken it, were toiling on without her help at least, and commonly against her endeavours. But I observed, when they approached to the barren top, that few were able to proceed without some support from Habit: and that they, whose Habits were strong, advanced towards the mists with little emotion, and entered them at last with calmness and confidence; after which, they were seen only by the eye of Religion; and though Reason looked after them with the most earnest curiosity, she could only obtain a faint glimpse, when her mistress, to enlarge her prospect, raised her from the ground. Reason, however, discerned that they were safe, but Religion saw that they were happy.

"Now, Theodore," said my protector, "withdraw thy view from the regions of obscurity, and see the fate of those who, when they were dismissed by Education, would admit no direction but that of Reason. Survey their wanderings, and be wise."

I looked then upon the Road of Reason, which was indeed, so far as it reached, the same with that of Religion, nor had Reason discovered it but by her instruction. Yet when she had once been taught it, she clearly saw that it was right; and Pride had sometimes incited her to declare that she discovered it herself, and persuaded her to offer herself as a guide to Religion; whom after many vain experiments she found it her highest privilege to follow. Reason was however at last well instructed in part of the way, and appeared to teach it with some success, when her precepts were not misrepresented by Passion, or her influence overborne by Appetite. But neither of these enemies was she able to resist. When Passion seized upon her votaries, she seldom attempted opposition: she seemed indeed to contend with more vigour against Appetite, but was generally overwearied in the contest; and if either of her opponents had confederated with Habit, her authority was wholly at an end. When Habit endeavoured to captivate the votaries of Religion, she grew by slow degrees, and gave time to escape; but in seizing the unhappy followers of Reason, she proceeded as one that had nothing to fear, and enlarged her size, and doubled her chains without intermission, and without reserve.

The whispers of Ambition

Of those who forsook the directions of Reason, some were led aside by the whispers of Ambition, who was perpetually pointing to stately palaces, situated on eminences on either side, recounting the delights of affluence, and boasting the security of power. They were easily persuaded to follow her, and Habit quickly threw her chains upon them; they were soon convinced of the folly of their choice, but few of them attempted to return. Ambition led them forward from precipice to precipice, where many fell and were seen no more.

Those that escaped were, after a long series of hazards, generally delivered over to Avarice, and enlisted by her in the service of Tyranny, where they continued to heap up gold till their patrons or their heirs pushed them headlong at last into the caverns of Despair.

Others were enticed by Intemperance to ramble in search of those fruits that hung over the rocks, and filled the air with their fragrance. I observed, that the Habits which hovered about these soon grew to an enormous size, nor were there any who less attempted to return to Reason, or sooner sunk into the gulfs that lay before them.

When these first quitted the road, Reason looked after them with a frown of contempt, but had little expectations of being able to reclaim them; for the bowl of intoxication was of such qualities as to make them lose all regard but for the present moment; neither Hope nor Fear could enter their retreats; and Habit had so absolute a power, that even Conscience, if Religion had employed her in their favour, would not have been able to force an entrance.

There were others whose crime it was rather to neglect Reason than to disobey her; and who retreated from the heat and tumult of the way, not to the bowers of Intemperance, but to the maze of Indolence.

They had this peculiarity in their condition, that they were always in sight of the Road of Reason, always wishing for her presence, and always resolving to return tomorrow.

In these was most eminently conspicuous the subtlety of Habit, who hung imperceptible shackles upon them, and was every moment leading them farther from the road, which they always imagined that they had the power of reaching.

They wandered on from one double of the labyrinth to another with the chains of Habit hanging secretly upon them, till, as they advanced, the flowers grew paler, and the scents fainter; they proceeded in their dreary march without pleasure in their progress, yet without power to return; and had this aggravation above all others, that they were criminal but not delighted.

Intemperance

Indolence and Despair

The drunkard for a time laughed over his wine; the ambitious man triumphed in the miscarriage of his rival; but the captives of Indolence had neither superiority nor merriment.

Discontent lowered in their looks, and Sadness hovered round their shades; yet they crawled on reluctant and gloomy, till they arrived at the depth of the recess, varied only with poppies and nightshade, where the dominion of Indolence terminates, and the hopeless wanderer is delivered up to Melancholy; the chains of Habit are rivetted for ever; and Melancholy, having tortured her prisoner for a time, consigns him at last to the cruelty of Despair.

While I was musing on this miserable scene, my protector called out to me, "Remember, Theodore, and be wise, and let not Habit prevail against thee." I started, and beheld myself surrounded by the rocks of Teneriffe: the birds of light were singing in the trees, and the glances of the morning darted upon me.

The Awakening, the Birds of Light

Epilogue by Stefka Ritchie

*Frontispiece, The Gentleman's
Magazine, Vol. XVII (1747)*

I therefore, resolved to devote the rest of my life to curiosity, and without any confinement of my excursions or termination of my views, to wander over the boundless regions of general knowledge (*Rambler* 177).

Perceived as a whole, Johnson's scepter of criticism vibrates in all its parts with colour and light, allowing for a continuous variation of our pictorial reconstruction of it. The affinity between text and image remains a prominent feature of post-Newtonian eighteenth-century art, and this is confirmed by Johnson who spoke of the resemblance between poetry and painting, 'two arts which pursue the same end, by the operation of the same mental faculties and which differ only as the one represents things by marks permanent and material, the other by signs accidental and arbitrary'. And if painting is 'more easily and generally understood', as it is 'immediately perceived', literature is 'capable of conveying more ideas' (*Idler* 34).

Johnson's manifesto for the role of the writer, delivered through Imlac in *Rasselas* is also a covenant with a universal appeal. In engaging with the living world, one must observe 'the power of all the passions in all their combinations' whose task is to 'trace the changes of the human mind as they are modified by various institutions and accidental influences of climate or custom'. But most of all the poet 'must write as the interpreter of nature, and the legislator of mankind, and consider himself as presiding over the thoughts and manners of future generations as being superior to time and place'. In other words, the writer for Johnson is a citizen of the world, a sentiment expressed forcefully by Francis Bacon who saw the goodness of man in the universal values of human nature, that is 'no island cut off from other lands, but a continent that joins to them' ('Of Goodness and Goodness of Nature'). As a man of his time, Johnson also employed the Newtonian concepts of dynamics to the prevailing taste of the beautiful and the vast in aesthetics; and in choosing to write about the general, he reached for the abstracted and invariable state of those universal truths which remain untouched by the passage of time.

'The business of the poet', says Imlac emphatically, 'is to examine, not the individual, but the species; to remark general properties and large appearances' – the permanent values in the context of the universal tangible reality. Seemingly over-enthusiastic on the surface, the statement contains the essence of Johnson's methodological approach as a writer, a survey of 'general properties and large appearances' and neglect of minute discriminations. Thus, his allegories can be viewed as a survey of those prominent and striking features of human nature which defy race, gender and national frontiers, recalling 'the original to mind' (*Rasselas*). Scanning his vast bank of knowledge from the books of the ancients, from Plato, Plutarch, Xenaphon and Pythagoras to Virgil, Horace, Cicero and Quintilian; and to those of the moderns, from Kepler and Descartes to Newton, Locke, Addison and Hogarth amongst many others. And through the creative process of the readers' personal experiences of discovery, Johnson reached out for the general truth. He instructs the future writer that 'if the topics be probable and persuasory, that he be able to recommend them by the superaddition of elegance and imagery, to display the colours of varied diction and pour forth the music of modulated periods', then he may refer to the beauty and sublimity of nature. It is Nature that evokes ideas which it forces upon the mind, conjuring up images of 'the sublime, the dreadful, and the vast' (*The Adventurer* 115).

Where now?

Today, with the unlimited potentials of the microchip and satellites continuously orbiting the sky, the 'microscope' and the 'telescope' have lost the lustre they would have had in the seventeenth and eighteenth centuries. Personifications, so much in vogue in the eighteenth century are no longer a favoured literary mode. This is yet another indication that ideas are not fossils, but evolving organisms as they focus on the outlook of people who epitomise a way of thinking – active, mobile, changing – a living embodiment of the sensibilities of an age. Further still, due to the advancement of the various disciplines of science today, its fragmentation into completely separate areas of research has reached irreversible proportions. Thus, science is often being perceived by the lay person as too analytic, thus unimaginative and detached from the mode of everyday life.

At the time of Johnson's death in 1784, a new era was breaking on the horizon, setting the scene for new strides in many key areas of scientific development. If in his day, 'science' meant learning or knowledge, and was part of Bacon's and Newton's natural philosophy, and it had a profound influence on the arts, in the nineteenth century, the inevitable increase of experimental and theoretical knowledge was already leading to their segregation. From the steam engine of James Watt to Thomas Young's longitudinal waves theory of light, Lamark's zoological philosophy and Cuvier's fossil theory of catastrophism, to Faraday's demonstrations on electrical forces, Schwann's cell theory and Darwin's theory of evolution – new discoveries were enlarging human knowledge of the workings of the universe. As various disciplines of science were becoming more narrowly defined, so was the artist's outlook – a far cry from the vast embrace of the eighteenth-century poetic vision of Pope Akenside, Addison, Thomson, Savage and Johnson.

It needs to be remembered that the eighteenth century is a direct inheritor of the investigative technique of Francis Bacon in the advancement of knowledge as the most promising method of improving humanity's lot. But to Bacon's conceived idea of experimental science as a collaborative enterprise, guided by a strictly laid out procedure, are juxtaposed the achievements of Isaac Newton, a solitary scholar whose knowledge and intuition had contributed to the formulations of the universal laws of nature. Through his writings Samuel Johnson insisted that in order to evaluate the history of mankind, one would have to look attentively at the peculiar character of each age. And when he appeals to the judgement of his readers, be it as a poet, writer of periodical essays and dedications, book reviewer or lexicographer, he is invoking common principles and shared expectations.

Thus, in order to gain deeper understanding of Johnson's mode of thinking, we must be aware of Bacon's and Newton's models of thinking as they transformed the whole outlook of future generations. Johnson's respect for the empirical fact inclined him toward a similar view to Bacon who argued for truthful representation of facts in the advancement of knowledge. But Newton's revolutionary ideas of colour and light, and matter in motion appealed to the creative impulse of his artistic imagination. Their philosophies are to be studied not for the sake of any definite answers but rather for the questions they pose – they enlarge our conception of what is possible, enrich our intellectual imagination; and as they diminish out dogmatic assurance which closes the mind against speculation, they bring us closer to the 'real' Johnson. It will allow us to rise above the mediocre and trivial detail permitting a survey of his works from a loftier position.

The universal appeal of Johnson's allegories needs to be highlighted. As Johnson puts this clearly through Imlac in *Rasselas*, 'the business of a poet is to examine, not the individual, but the species; to remark general properties and large appearances'. His task was to 'trace the changes of the human mind as they are modified by various institutions and accidental influences of climate or custom. But most of all, the poet 'must write as the interpreter of nature, and the legislator of mankind, and consider himself as presiding over the thoughts and manners of future generations; as being superior to time and place' (*Rasselas*). In his allegories Johnson reached to the treasures of the ancients choosing from the Greeks and the Romans their ability to lend allegorical significance to their figures through a single attribute and look up to the wisdom of the East. From Shakespeare he learned how to create his characters unmodified by the custom of particular places that is not practised by the rest of the world. As a man of his time, he employed the prevailing tastes in aesthetics that embraced Bacon's pragmatism and Newton's universal concepts of science. As he scanned his vast bank of knowledge from the books of the ancients and those of the moderns, Johnson sought the active participation of the reader in a creative process of self-discovery. And the figure that emerges is more exciting, more vibrant and complex, and certainly more akin to the 'real' Johnson who truly shared the sensibilities of his Age, with perpetual curiosity in pursuit of learning and self-improvement for the betterment of society as a whole.

Photo Art image, 'In the Advancement of Knowledge', by Svetlan Stefanov

BIBLIOGRAPHY

For the Introduction by Barbara Fogarty

Barthes, Roland, 'Rhetoric of the Image' (1964) in *Image, Music, Text*, London: Fontana Press, 1977, pp. 32-51.
Brown, John, *John Bunyan: His Life, Times and Works*, 1909 [online]. Available on: https://www.archive.org/stream/johnbunyanhislif01browuoft. [Accessed 16 March 2015].
Holmes, Richard, *The Age of Wonder: How the Romantic Generation Discovered the Beauty and Terror of Science*, London: HarperCollins, 2008.
Johnson, Gary, *The Vitality of Allegory: Figural narrative in Modern and Contemporary Fiction*, 2012.
Johnson,Samuel,*IdlerNo.34*[online].Available on:
http://www.readbookonline.net/readOnLine/29940. [Accessed 16 March 2015].
Reynolds, Joshua, *Sir Joshua Reynolds's Discourses*, Vol. I and Vol. II, publ. by John Sharpe, 1820.
Ritchie, Stefka, 'Samuel Johnson in an Age of Science', unpublished M Phil thesis, University of Central England (UCE), Birmingham, UK, 2002.
Ritchie, Stefka, 'Celebrating Dr Johnson: Words are Images of things', unpublished paper, 2010.
Rogers, Pat, *Oxford Dictionary of National Biography*, 'Samuel Johnson (1709-1784), author and lexicographer' [online]. Available on: http://www.oxforddnb.com. [Accessed 7 March 2015].
Turner, Jane (ed.), *The Grove Dictionary of Art*, 2003; Peter Paul Rubens, Marc Chagall, William Hogarth, Joshua Reynolds.
Vaughan, William, *British Painting: The Golden Age from Hogarth to Turner*, London: Thames & Hudson, 1999.

Foreword, Analytical Notes and Epilogue by Stefka Ritchie

Printed Works by Samuel Johnson
The Complete English Poems, ed. J D Fleeman (Harmondsworth: Penguin Books, 1971).
A Dictionary of the English Language, 2 vols (1755). First Folio Edition.
A Dictionary of the English Language, 2 vols (1773). Fourth edition. A Dictionary of the English Language, CD-Rom, ed. Anne McDermott (Cambridge: CUP, 1996).
A Journey to the Western Islands of Scotland, ed. J D Fleeman (Oxford: Clarendon Press, 1985).
The Letters of Samuel Johnson, with Mrs Thrale's Genuine Letters to Him, ed. R W Chapman, 3 vols. (Oxford: Clarendon Press, 1952).
The Letters of Samuel Johnson, ed. Bruce Redford, 5 vols. (Princeton: Princeton University Press, 1993).
Lives of the English Poets, ed. G B Hill, 3 vols (Oxford: Clarendon Press, 1905).
The Works of Samuel Johnson, 9 vols (London and Oxford: Talboys and Pickering, 1825).
'Preface' to the *Preceptor*, Vol. IV, pp. 244; 'Preface to the English Dictionary', Vol. V, pp. 23-51.
'Plan of A Dictionary of the English Language', Vol. V, pp. 5-22.
The Yale Edition of the Works of Samuel Johnson. 24 vols. (New Haven and London: Yale University Press, 1958-).

Journals
The Gentleman's Magazine (1738-1756)
The Literary Magazine (1756-1758)

Other Printed Primary Sources
Bacon, Francis, Lord Verulam, *The Works of Francis Bacon*, ed. J Spedding, R L Ellis and D D Heath, 14 vols; first publ. 1857-74 (London: Longman & Co, rev. ed. 1883-94).
Bacon, Francis, Vol. IV (1883), *The Great Instauration*, pp. 5-38. 'Preface', pp. 13-21; Plan of the Work', pp. 22-33, *The New Organon*, pp. 39-248; 'Preface', pp. 39-43; Book I, pp. 47-117, Book ii, pp. 119-248, *Of the Dignity of Learning*, Book ii, pp. 275-498.
Boswell, James. *Life of Johnson*, ed. G B Hill, rev. L F Powell, 6 vols (Oxford, 1934, rept. 1971).
Boswell, James. *Life of Johnson*, ed. R W Chapman, (unabridged). Introduction by Pat Rogers, first publ. 1980 (Oxford: OUP, 1998).

Burke, Edmund. *A Philosophical Enquiry into the Origin of our Ideas of the Sublime and Beautiful* (1757; Oxford: Oxford World's Classics, OUP, 2008).
A Catalogue of the valuable Library of Books of the late learned Samuel Johnson Esq, LLD (1892) reprinted for the Meeting of the Johnson Club at Oxford, June 11, with notes by John Courtenay, 1786.
Cook. William. *The Life of Samuel Johnson, LLD, with Occasional Remarks on His Writings; An Authentic Copy of his Will; A Catalogue of His Works, and a Facsimile of his Handwriting* (London: Kearsley,1785).
Hawkins, John. *The Life of Samuel Johnson, LLD* (London, 1787).
Hogarth, William. *The Analysis of Beauty*, ed. with introduction and notes by Ronald Paulson (1753; The Paul Mellon Centre for the Study of British Art, 1997).
Johnsonian Miscellanies, ed. George Birkbeck-Hill, 2 vols, first publ. 1897 (New York: Barnes & Noble and London: Constable, rept. 1970).
Anecdotes of the late Samuel Johnson, LLD by Hester Thrale Lynch Piozzi, Vol. I, pp. 141-350.
An Essay on the Life and Genius of Samuel Johnson. LLD by Arthur Murphy, Vol. I, pp. 355-488.
Life of Johnson, by George Kearsley, Vol. II, pp. 161-71.
MacLaurin, Colin. *An Account of Sir Isaac Newton's Philosophical Discoveries* (London, 1750).
The Methods of Fluxions and Infinite Series with its application to the geometry of Curve-Lines by the Inventor Sir Isaac Newton. Translation from the Author's Latin Original, not yet made publick, with a perpetual comment upon the whole Work by John Colson, FRS (London: Henry Woodgall, 1733).
The Natural Philosophy of Sir Isaac Newton and His System of the World [Principia]. Translated by Andrew Motte (1729). The translations revised and supplied with an Historical and explanatory appendix, by Florian Cajori, 2 vols. (Berkeley & Los Angeles: University of California Press, 1966).
Pemberton, Henry, *A View of Sir Isaac Newton's Philosophy* (London, 1728).
Piozzi, H T. *Autobiography, Letters and Literary Remains of Mrs Piozzi (Thrale)*, 2 vols, ed. A Hayward (London: Longman and Roberts, 2nd ed).
Thrale, Hester. *Thraliana – The diary of Mrs Hester Lynch Thrale*, 2 vols (London: Longman and Roberts, 1861).
A Treatise of the Reflections, *Refractions, Inflections, and Colours of Light* (*Opticks*). With a Forward by Albert Einstein, and an Introduction by E T Whittaker (London: G Bell, 1931; reprt. From the fourth ed., 1730).
Unpublished Scientific Papers of Isaac Newton, ed. A Rupert Hall and Marie Boas Hall (CUP, 1962).

Secondary Sources
Books
Abbott, J L and Allan, D G C *(eds)*. *The Virtuoso Tribe of Arts and Sciences: Studies in the Eighteenth-Century Work and Membership of the London Society of Arts* (Athens: Univ. of Georgia Press, 1992).
Albee, E. *A History of English Utilitarianism* (London: Swan Sonnenschein; New York, Macmillan, 1902).
Alkon, P. *Samuel Johnson and moral discipline* (Evanston: Northwestern University Press, 1967).
Allan, D G C. William Shipley, founder of the Royal Society of Arts: a biography with documents (London: Scolar Press, 1979).
Allen, R C. *The British Industrial Revolution in Global Perspective* (CUP, 2009).
Bate, W J. *The Achievements of Samuel Johnson* (New York: OUP, 1955).
Bate, W J. *Samuel Johnson* (New York: Harcourt Brace Jovanovich, 1977).
Bloom, E, A. *Samuel Johnson in Grub Street* (Providence, RI: Brown University Press, 1957).
Brewer, J, *English Culture in the Eighteenth Century* (Chicago: The University of Chicago Press, 1997).
Briggs, A. *The Age of Improvement 1783-1867*, first publ. 1959 (London: Longman, 2000, 2nd ed).
Bronowski, H, J. *The Ascent of Man* (London: BBC series, 1973).
Brownell, M R. *Samuel Johnson's Attitude to the Arts* (Oxford: Clarendon Press, 1989).
Caine, B. *History and Biography* (Basingstoke: Palgrave Macmillan, 2010).
Carlyle, T. *Samuel Johnson* (London, 1853).
The Cambridge History of Eighteenth-Century Political Thought, (eds). M Goldie and R D Walker, (CUP, 2006).

Carr, E H. *What is History?* (London: Macmillan, 1961).
Christianson, G E. *Isaac Newton and His Times.* (New York: The Free Press, 1984).
Clark, J C D and Erskine-Hill, H. *Samuel Johnson in historical context* (London: Palgrave Macmillan, 2002).
Clark, J C D and Erskine-Hill, H (eds). *The Interpretation of Samuel Johnson* (London: Macmillan, 2012).
Clifford, J L and Greene, D J. *Samuel Johnson: A Survey and Bibliography of Critical Studies* (Minneapolis: University of Minnesota Press, 1970).
Clifford, J L. *Dictionary Johnson* (New York: McGraw-Hall, 1979).
Clingham, G and Smallwood P (eds). *Samuel Johnson after 300 Years* (CUP, 2009).
Courtney, W P. *A Bibliography of Samuel Johnson* (Oxford: Clarendon Press, 1915).
Cowan, A and **Steward, J**. *The City and the Senses: Urban Culture since 1500* (Aldershot: Ashgate Press, 2006).
DeMaria, R. *Johnson's Dictionary and the Language of Learning* (Chapel Hill: University of North Carolina Press, 1986).
DeMaria, R. *The Life of Samuel Johnson: A Critical Biography* (Oxford: Blackwell, 1993).
Dunn, J. *The political thought of John Locke: an historical account* (CUP, 1995).
Eddy, D. *Samuel Johnson. Book Reviewer in the Literary Magazine: or, Universal Review 1756-1758*, 4 vols. (New York & London: Garland Publ, 1979).
Eddy, D and Fleeman, J D. *A preliminary handlist of books to which Dr Samuel Johnson subscribed* (Charlottesville: Bibliographical Society of the University of Virginia, 1993).
Gaukroger, S. *Francis Bacon and the Transformation of Modern Philosophy* (CUP, 2001).
Greene, D. *The Age of Exuberance: Background to Eighteenth-Century English Literature* (New York, 1970).
Greene, D. *The Politics of Samuel Johnson* (New Haven: YUP, 1960; 1990, 2nd rev. ed).
Fleeman, D J D. *A Bibliography of the Works of Samuel Johnson, Treating His Published Works from the Beginnings to 1984*, 2 vols. (Oxford: Clarendon Press, 2000).
Fitzpatrick, M and Jones, P. *The Enlightenment World* (New York & London: Routledge, 2004).
Friedel, R. *A Culture of Improvement* (Cambridge, Mass.: MIT Press, 2007).
Fussell, P. *Samuel Johnson and the Life of Writing* (NY: Harcourt, 1971).
Hampson, N. *The Enlightenment: An Evaluation of Its Assumptions, Attitudes and Values* (Harmondsworth: Penguin Books, 1968).
Hanley, B. *Samuel Johnson as a Book Reviewer. A Duty to Examine the Labors of the Learned* (Newark: University of Delaware Press & London: Associated University Presses, 2011).
Hazen, A T. *Samuel Johnson's Prefaces and Dedications*, first publ. 1937 (New Haven, Conn: Kennikat Press, rept. 1973).
Holmes, R. *Dr Johnson and Mr Savage*, first publ. 1993 (London: Harper Perennial, 2005, 2nd ed).
Hudson, D and K W Luckhurst. *The Royal Society of Arts* (London: John Murray, 1954).
Hudson, N. *Samuel Johnson and Eighteenth-Century Thought* (Oxford: OUP, 1988).
Jolley N. *Locke: His Philosophical Thought* (Oxford: OUP, 1999).
Kaminski T. *The Early Career of Samuel Johnson* (Oxford: OUP, 1987).
Katritzky, L. *Johnson and the Letters of Junius: New Perspectives on an Old Enigma* (New York: Peter Lang, 1996).
Keach, B. *Preaching from the Type and Metaphors of the Bible* (Grand Rapids, Mich: Kregel, 1972).
Knox, R A. *Caliban in Grub Street* (London: Sheed & Ward,1930).
Langford, P. *A polite and commercial society 1722-1783*, first publ. 1989 (OUP, 1998).
Langford, P. *The Eighteenth-Century* ed. Paul Langford (OUP, 2002).
Lipking, L. *Samuel Johnson: The Life of an Author* (Cambridge, MA: HUP, 1998).
Losonsky, M. *Linguistic Turns in Modern Philosophy* (CUP, 2006).
Lynch, J (ed). *Samuel Johnson in Context* (Cambridge: CUP, 2012).
Lynn, S. *Samuel Johnson after Deconstruction* (Carbondale and Edwardsville: Southern Illinois University Press, 1992).
Martin, P. *Samuel Johnson: A Biography* (Cambridge, MA.: HUP, 2008); rpt. (London: Weidenfeld & Nicolson, 2009).
McIntyre, A. *After Virtue: A Study in Moral Philosophy* (London: Duckworth, 1985, 2nd ed).
Miller, Arthur. *Insights of Genius* (New York: Springer Verlag, 1996).
Morris, C W (ed). *The Social Contract Theorists: Critical Essays on Hobbes, Locke, and Rousseau* (Lanham, MD: Rowman and Littlefield, 1999).
Nichols, J. *Literary Anecdotes of the Eighteenth Century*, 9 vols (London, 1812-16).

Nicolson, Marjorie Hope. *Newton demands the Muse: Newton's Opticks and the Eighteenth-Century Poets* (Westport, Conn: Greewood Press, 1946).
Nokes, D. *Samuel Johnson: A Life* (London: Faber & Faber, 2009).
Porter, R. *The Creation of the Modern World* (New York and London: W W Norton, 2000).
Reddick, A. *The Making of Johnson's Dictionary, 1746-1773*; first publ. 1990 (Cambridge & New York: CUP, rev.1996).
Rogers, P. *Samuel Johnson* (Oxford: OUP, 1993).
Rogers, P. *The Samuel Johnson Encyclopedia* (Westport, CT: Greenwood Press, 1996).
Schwartz, Joseph. *The Creative Moment* (London: Jonathan Cape, 1992).
Schwartz, R, *Samuel Johnson and the New Science* Madison, Wisc.: The University of Wisconsin Press, 1971).
Spadafora, D. *The Idea of Progress in the Eighteenth-Century Britain* (New Haven & London: YUP, 1990).
Spector, R D. *Samuel Johnson and the Essay* (Westport, Conn: Greenwood Press, 1997).
Sorenzen, Roy A. *Thought Experiments* (Oxford: 1992).
Voitle, R. *Samuel Johnson the Moralist* (Cambridge, Mass: Harvard University Press, 1961).
Westfall, Richard, S. *Never at Rest* | (Cambridge: CUP, 1980).
Wimsatt, W K. *Philosophic Words. A Study of Style and Meaning in the Rambler and Dictionary of Samuel Johnson* (Yale: Yale University Press, 1948; rept. Archon Books, 1968).
Wood, H T. *History of the Royal Society of Arts* (London, 1913).

Articles and Chapters in Books
Aarsleff, A. 'Locke's Reputation in Nineteenth-Century England' in *From Locke to Saussure* (Minneapolis: Univ. of Minnesota Press, 1982), pp. 120-45.
Aarsleff, A. 'The State of Nature and the Nature of Man in Locke,' in *John Locke: Problems and Perspectives*, ed. John W. Yolton (CUP, 1969), pp. 99-136.
Abbott, J. 'Johnson's Membership of the Society reconsidered', *RSA Journal* (August 1985), Vol. 133; pp. 618-622.
Abbott, J. 'Dr Johnson and the Society', *RSA Journal,* Parts I, II (CXV) (1967), pp. 395- 400; pp. 486-91.
Abbott, J L and **Allan, D G C**. '"Compassion and Horror in Every Humane Mind": Samuel Johnson, the Society of Arts, and Eighteenth Century Prostitution,' *RSA Jnl*, Vol. 136 (1988): pp. 749–54, pp. 827–32. Reprinted in *The Virtuoso Tribe of Arts and Sciences: Studies in the Eighteenth-Century Work and Membership of the London Society of Arts*, (eds) **Allan D G C** and **Abbott, J L** (Athens: Univ. of Georgia Press, 1992), pp. 18–37.
Allan, D C. (i) 'Notions of Economic Policy Expressed by the Society's Correspondents and in its Publications 1754-1847', *RSA Jnl*, Vol. 106, (Sept. 1958), pp. 800-804; (ii) 'The Employments of the Poor and the Preservation of the Structure of Society', (December 1958), pp. 55-59.
Brack, O M Jr. 'The works of Samuel Johnson and the canon' in *Samuel Johnson after 300 Years'*, (eds) Clingham, G and Smallwood, P (CUP, 2009), pp. 246-283.
Buickerood, James. 'Pursuing the Science of Man: Some Difficulties in Understanding Eighteenth Century Maps of the Mind', *Eighteenth-Century Life* 19 (May 1995), pp. 1-17.
Clark, J C D. 'The Cultural Identity of Samuel Johnson', *The Age of Johnson: A Scholarly Annual* 8 (1997), pp. 15–70.
Clifford, J L. 'Further Letters of the Johnson Circle', *Bulletin of the John Ryland Library*, Vol. XX (July-August 1936), pp. 280-82.
Clifford, J L. 'Johnson and the Society of Artists' in *The Augustan Milieu: Essays Presented to Louis A Landa*, (eds). Miller, H K, Rothstein, E and Rousseau, G S (Oxford: Clarendon Press, 1970), pp. 333-348.
Clingham G. 'Johnson now and in time' in *Samuel Johnson after 300 Years*, (eds) Clingham, G and Smallwood, P (Cambridge: CUP, 2009), pp. 1-15.
Cochrane, R C. 'Francis Bacon and the use of the Mechanical Arts', *Annals of Science*, 12, pp. 137-156.
Curley T M. 'Johnson's Secret Collaboration' in *The Unknown Samuel Johnson*, (eds) Burke, J J Jr and Kay, D (Madison: University of Wisconsin Press, 1983).
DeMaria R. 'The eighteenth-century periodical essay' in *The Cambridge History of English Literature 1660-1780*, (ed) John Richetti (CUP, 2004), pp. 525-548.
Donaldson, Ian. 'Samuel Johnson and the Art of Observation', *English Language Studies* (ELS), 53 (4) (Winter 1986), pp. 779-99.

Gramsci, A. 'Observations on Folklore: '"Natural Law" and Folklore' in *Selections from the Cultural Writings*, ed. D Forgacs and G Nowell-Smith (Cambridge, Mass.: HUP, 1985), pp. 193-224.

Hendrick, E. 'Locke's Theory of Language and Johnson's *Dictionary*, *Eighteenth-Century Studies*, Vol. 20 (1987), pp. 420-44.

Hesse, Mary. 'Francis Bacon's Philosophy of Science' in *Essential Articles for the Study of Francis Bacon*, ed. Brian Vickers (London: Sedgwick & Jackson, 1972), pp. 107-139.

Johnson, C L. 'Samuel Johnson's Moral Psychology and Locke's "Of Power"', *SEL*, Vol. 24 (1984), pp. 564-582.

Kolb, G J and Kolb, R A. 'The Selection and Use of the Illustrative Quotations in Dr. Johnson's Dictionary' in *New Aspects of Lexicography*, (ed) Weinbrot, H D (Carbondale: Southern Illinois Univ. Press, 1972), pp 61-72.

Korshin, P J. 'Johnson, the Essay and *The Rambler*' in *The Cambridge Companion to Samuel Johnson*, (ed) Clingham, G (Cambridge: CUP), pp. 51-67.

Lynn, S. 'Johnson's Critical Reception' in *The Cambridge Companion to Samuel Johnson*, (ed) Clingham, G (Cambridge: CUP, 1997), pp. 240-253.

Macaulay, Lord. 'Life of Johnson' in *Johnson's Chief Lives from Johnson's Lives of the English Poets*, edited with "Preface" by Matthew Arnold, first publ. 1881 (New York: Russell & Russell, rept. 1968), pp. 1-42.

MacLaverty, J, 'From Definition to Explanation: Locke's influence on Johnson's *Dictionary*, *Journal of the History of Ideas*, Vol. 47 (1986), pp. 377-394.

Oakley, F. 'Locke, natural Law and God: Again' in *History of Political Thought*, Vol. 17 (1997), pp. 624-51.

Parker, F. "We are perpetually moralists": Johnson and moral philosophy' in *Johnson after 300 years*, (eds) Clingham, G and Smallwood, P (Cambridge: CUP, 2009), pp. 15-32.

Stephen, L. 'Dr Johnson's Writings' in *Hours in a Library* (London: Putman, 1904), Vol. 2, pp. 1-18.

Troy, F S. 'Samuel Johnson in Modern Perspective' in *Biography & Criticisms* (The Massachusetts Review, 1978), pp. 517-41.

Woodruff, J F. 'Johnson's *Rambler* and Its Contemporary Context', *Bulleting of Research in the Humanities*, No 85, (1982), pp. 27-64.

Illustrations

Cover design by Svetlan Stefanov

A Sketch of Samuel Johnson (after Joshua Reynolds, 1769) by Svetlan Stefanov

Rambler 3
1 Frontispiece (*Gents Mag., Vol. XX 1750*)	25
2 Prelude to *Rambler* 3, by Svetlan Stefanov	33

Illustrations by Ana Stefanova
3 Criticism in the palace of Wisdom	35
4 The Scepter of Criticism	36
5 The Torch of Truth	38
6 Criticism descends with the Muses	39
7 The distorted Parts of the Whole	40
8 The destructive Force of the Poppies	41
9 The action of Time	42
10 Criticism leaves Earth. The False Torch	43
11 The Time decides	44

Rambler 22
12 Frontispiece (*Gents Mag., Vol. XVII 1747*)	45
13 Prelude to *Rambler* 22, by Svetlan Stefanov	50

Illustrations by Ana Stefanova
14 Wit and Learning	52
15 The Rivals harass each other	53
16 Wit protected by Venus and Learning, the favourite of Minerva	54
17 Wit, Malice and their son Satyr	54
18 Wit and Learning amongst the Mortals	55
19 Pluto, the god of Riches	56
20 Wit and Learning readmitted by Jupiter	57
21 The Marriage of Wit and Learning	58

Rambler 33
22 Frontispiece (*Gents Mag., Vol. XXI 1751*)	59
23 Prelude to *Rambler* 33, by Svetlan Stefanov	64

Illustrations by Ana Stefanova
24 In the early Ages	65
25 The Fall	66
26 Labour, the son of Necessity, the pupil of Art	67
27 Lassitude	69
28 Luxury lets in Disease, Satiety and Lassitude	70
29 Health, the daughter of Labour and Rest	71

Rambler 65
30 Frontispiece (*Gents Mag., Vol. XIX 1749*)	72
31 Prelude to *Rambler* 65, by Svetlan Stefanov	77

Illustrations by Ana Stefanova
32 The Morning	78
33 Obidah on the Hills	79
34 The Sunset	80
35 The power of Nature	81
36 The air grew blacker	82
37 In the cradle of the night	83
38 The Morning is still to come	84
39 In the steps of the Old Man	86

Rambler 67
40 Frontispiece (*Gents Mag., Vol. XXV 1755*) ... 87
41 Prelude to *Rambler* 67, by Svetlan Stefanov ... 92
Illustrations by Ana Stefanova
42 Hope ... 93
43 The Dream ... 95
44 The chains of Slavery ... 96
45 Science ... 97
46 At the gates of Fancy and Reason ... 100
47 The two Beasts ... 101
48 The Awakening from a Nightmare (Il.S. Stefanov) ... 102

Rambler 102
49 Frontispiece (*Gents Mag., Vol. XXV 1755*) ... 103
50 Prelude to *Rambler* 102, by Svetlan Stefanov ... 107
Illustrations by Ana Stefanova
51 The years of Manhood ... 108
52 The Voyage of Life ... 109
53 In the course of the Voyage of Life ... 110
54 The Gulph of Intemperance ... 112
55 The Rocks of Pleasure ... 113
56 The Sudden Awakening ... 114

The Vision of Theodore
57 Frontispiece (after L S Lowry, 1943) by Stefka Ritchie ... 115
58 Prelude to *The Vision of Theodore*, by Svetlan Stefanov ... 127
Illustrations by Ana Stefanova
59 The Hermit in his cell ... 128
60 The Rocks of Teneriffe ... 130
61 I sat down to rest ... 131
62 I heard the sound as of the flight of eagles ... 133
63 The Mountain of Existence ... 134
64 In the Path of Education ... 136
65 Temptations ... 138
66 Reason, the noblest and the greatest ... 139
67 Religion ... 141
69 The bondage of Habits ... 143
70 The Road of Happiness ... 145
71 The whispers of Ambition ... 147
72 Intemperance ... 149
73 Indolence and Despair ... 150
74 The Awakening, the Birds of Light ... 152

Epilogue
75 Frontispiece (*Gents. Mag. Vol. XXIV 1754*) ... 153
76 Photo Art, *In the Advancement of Knowledge*, by Svetlan Stefanov ... 156